Say the Word!

A Guide to Improving Word Recognition Skills

Barbara Rosenberg Loss

New Readers Press

Dedicated to Danny, Jackie, and Cal

In memory of my parents, Drs. Hans and Ernestine Rosenberg

Acknowledgments: I would like to acknowledge my teacher Dr. Lydia A. Duggins, whose insights into perceptual training and whose philosophy about human intelligence underlie this program. Also I would like to acknowledge my students who have taught me so much and for whose personal improvement I have developed this program. I would like to thank my colleagues and friends at Fairfield High School for their encouragement, and I am especially grateful to all of my family for their endless support.

— Barbara Rosenberg Loss

ISBN 978-0-88336-152-8

Copyright © 1991 New Readers Press
New Readers Press
A Publishing Division of ProLiteracy
1320 Jamesville Avenue, Syracuse, New York 13210
www.newreaderspress.com

Printed in the United States of America
20 19 18 17 16 15 14 13 12 11 10

All proceeds from the sale of New readers Press materials
support literacy programs in the United States and worldwide.

Editorial development, design, art, and composition by Publicom, Inc.

CONTENTS

PART 4 Word Beginnings and Endings 103

Word Beginnings

Word Endings

INTRODUCTION

Welcome to *Say the Word! A Guide to Improving Word Recognition Skills.* The purpose of this program is to improve your word recognition skills and to increase your speed of reading.

In *Say the Word!* you will learn about letter patterns that cause problems for many readers. You will learn some general rules that will help you read almost any new word. You will have many opportunities to apply your new skills to words in practice sentences.

About This Book

This student handbook is written so that you can study and learn with or without a teacher or tutor in the room with you. Everything you need is in the handbook — the instructional lessons plus many lists of words and sentences for practice and review.

Before you begin using the handbook, take a few minutes to become familiar with it.

- Look at the table of contents on pages 3-6. Get a feeling for the kinds of topics in the book and for how they are organized into parts. Notice where Mixed Reviews are found.

- Look at the Pronunciation Guide on page 11. This guide explains the respelling system and symbols that are used in this book. Letter sounds or words are often respelled to help you pronounce them. Within the lessons of this handbook, the symbols shown on page 11 are placed inside two slashes. For example, the sound of long *a* that you hear in the word *late* is shown this way: /ā/. The respelling for the entire word *feet* is shown in parentheses as (fēt). You may find it helpful to refer to the Pronunciation Guide often as you work through the lessons.

- Look at the Extra Practice section on pages 167-220. These pages give additional sentences for you to practice the skills you are learn-ing in each lesson.

- Look at the Appendix on pages 221-231. Those lists support and extend some of the lessons in the book.

The heart of the handbook is in the instructional lessons, organized into parts. You may want to start at the beginning of the handbook and work your way through to the end. You may want to focus only on the les-sons covering specific problem areas. Use this handbook in the way that best suits your own needs after they have been identified during sessions with your teacher or tutor.

- Look at the Part 3 introduction on page 87. Each part of the handbook begins with such a page. It shows what letter patterns are taught in the part, and it lists key words that have those letter patterns.

Every lesson within every part has a similar format. Become familiar with that format below.

A Typical Lesson

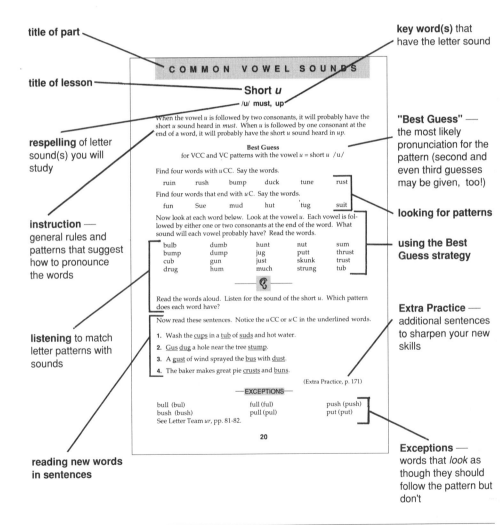

title of part — key word(s) that have the letter sound

title of lesson

COMMON VOWEL SOUNDS

Short u

/u/ must, up

When the vowel u is followed by two consonants, it will probably have the short u sound heard in *must*. When u is followed by one consonant at the end of a word, it will probably have the short u sound heard in *up*.

"Best Guess" — the most likely pronunciation for the pattern (second and even third guesses may be given, too!)

respelling of letter sound(s) you will study

Best Guess
for VCC and VC patterns with the vowel u = short u /u/

Find four words with uCC. Say the words.

| ruin | rush | bump | duck | tune | rust |

Find four words that end with uC. Say the words.

| fun | Sue | mud | hut | tug | suit |

looking for patterns

instruction — general rules and patterns that suggest how to pronounce the words

Now look at each word below. Look at the vowel u. Each vowel is followed by either one or two consonants at the end of the word. What sound will each vowel probably have? Read the words.

bulb	dumb	hunt	nut	sum
bump	dump	jug	putt	thrust
cub	gun	just	skunk	trust
drug	hum	much	strung	tub

using the Best Guess strategy

listening to match letter patterns with sounds

Read the words aloud. Listen for the sound of the short u. Which pattern does each word have?

Now read these sentences. Notice the uCC or uC in the underlined words.

1. Wash the <u>cups</u> in a <u>tub</u> of <u>suds</u> and hot water.
2. <u>Gus</u> <u>dug</u> a hole near the tree <u>stump</u>.
3. A <u>gust</u> of wind sprayed the <u>bus</u> with <u>dust</u>.
4. The baker makes great pie <u>crusts</u> and <u>buns</u>.

(Extra Practice, p. 171)

Extra Practice — additional sentences to sharpen your new skills

EXCEPTIONS

| bull (bul) | full (ful) | push (push) |
| bush (bush) | pull (pul) | put (put) |

See Letter Team ur, pp. 81-82.

20

reading new words in sentences

Exceptions — words that *look* as though they should follow the pattern but don't

Best Guess Strategy

The Best Guess in each lesson is a *general* rule. It identifies the *most likely* pronunciation for a letter pattern. But the most important ingredient in the Best Guess strategy is you, the student.

When you are trying to read a new word, use your common sense. Listen carefully. Do you hear a word you recognize when you use the Best Guess? If not, is there another way to say the letters? You must decide whether the Best Guess leads to the correct pronunciation in each new situation.

Getting Started

You already know that all letters are either vowels or consonants. The letters *a, e, i, o,* and *u* are always vowels, and the letter *y* is sometimes a vowel. All other letters are consonants.

Every word has at least one vowel. Vowels can be difficult to read because they can stand for more than one sound. Also, sometimes a vowel is heard by itself in a word and sometimes it is heard as part of a letter team.

Letter teams are pairs or groups of letters. A letter team may be made from two vowels, such as *ea*. Or it may be made from a vowel and a consonant, such as *aw*. Letter teams can also be made from two or more consonants, such as *tr* or *spl*.

Most consonants have only one sound. For this reason, they are usually easy to read. When you see the letter *b*, for instance, you know it almost always has the /b/ sound heard at the beginning and end of the word *bib*. Some consonants have more than one sound. For instance, the letter *c* can stand for different sounds. So can the letter *g*.

Many consonant teams blend the sounds of the consonants together. The letters *bl* sound like the /bl/ you hear at the beginning of the word *blue*. The letters *mp* sound like the /mp/ you hear at the end of *stomp*. Consonant teams can be found at the beginnings of words, as in *flag*. They can be found in the middle of words, as in *mister*. They can be found at the ends of words, as in *bank*. In the Appendix you can review different consonant teams.

Letter teams show up over and over again. So do certain patterns of vowels and consonants. These patterns are worth knowing because they can help you read many words. For example, many words have this pattern: a vowel, a consonant, a vowel. The words *ape* and *ice* follow this pattern. In this handbook, such patterns are written using a capital V for *vowel* and a capital C for *consonant*. So, the letters VCV mean a pattern that has a vowel, a consonant, a vowel. That pattern fits many words, for example:

VCV	VCV	VCV	VCV	VCV
ape	eve	ice	ode	use

In this book, you will learn many such patterns. They will help you read thousands of words.

PRONUNCIATION GUIDE

The sounds of different letters in different types of words are listed here. You may want to refer to this Pronunciation Guide often as you work through the lessons.

a	bat, back	j	jar, enjoy	u	up, must
ā	tale, wait	k	king, peek	u̇	full, put
ä	father, far	l	life, fool	ü	tune, due
		m	my, am		
b	boy, tab	n	new, on	v	very, save
ch	chip, such	ng	song, spring	w	want, washer
d	do, bed			y	yes, yard
		o	top, dock	z	zero, breeze
e	bed, test	ō	hope, toe	zh	measure,
ē	bead, see	ô	off, talk		seizure
ėr	term, learn	oi	boil, boy		
		ou	out, cow	ə represents:	
f	fog, if			a	in ago
g	get, sag	p	pepper, cap	e	in taken
h	hi, hot	r	ran, cry	i	in pencil
		s	see, yes	o	in wagon
i	did, bill	sh	she, push	u	in circus
ī	hike, lie	t	tan, pit		
		th	thin, both		
		ŦH	then, smooth		

PART 1 · COMMON VOWEL SOUNDS

The letters *a*, *e*, *i*, *o*, and *u* are called vowels. Sometimes the letter *y* is also a vowel.

Every word has at least one vowel. Vowels, though, can be hard to read. Each vowel can have different sounds. When vowels team up with each other, or with other letters, they have even more sounds.

Part 1 of the handbook will teach you the many sounds that vowels can have. It will show you when *y* is a vowel. Learning about vowels will help you read a great many words.

How many vowel sounds do you already know? Read the list below, continued on the next page. The key words will help you know the sounds that the vowels have.

back	/a/	page 16	boat	/ō/	page 26
bat	/a/	page 16	toe	/ō/	page 26
test	/e/	page 17	tune	/ü/	page 28
bed	/e/	page 17	suit	/ü/	page 28
bill	/i/	page 18	due	/ü/	page 28
did	/i/	page 18	cute	/yü/	page 28
dock	/o/	page 19	cue	/yü/	page 28
top	/o/	page 19	racket	/a/	page 32
must	/u/	page 20	dentist	/e/	page 33
up	/u/	page 20	silver	/i/	page 34
tale	/ā/	page 23	pocket	/o/	page 35
wait	/ā/	page 23	number	/u/	page 36
bead	/ē/	page 24	sailor	/ā/	page 37
see	/ē/	page 24	bacon	/ā/	page 37
hike	/ī/	page 25	seeing	/ē/	page 38
cried	/ī/	page 25	beater	/ē/	page 38
lie	/ī/	page 25	meter	/ē/	page 38
hope	/ō/	page 26	fiber	/ī/	page 39

boating	/ō/	page 40	comic	/o/	page 43
bonus	/ō/	page 40	punish	/u/	page 43
suitor	/ü/	page 42	ago	/ə/	page 45
cruel	/ü/	page 42	wagon	/ə/	page 45
prudent	/ü/	page 42	sky	/ī/	page 46
music	/yü/	page 42	apply	/ī/	page 46
cabin	/a/	page 43	style	/ī/	page 46
metal	/e/	page 43	tricky	/ē/	page 46
vivid	/i/	page 43	gym	/i/	page 46

Introduction to Short Vowels

Vowels have many sounds. One common sound that each vowel has is called the short sound. The short sound for *a*, for instance, is the sound you hear at the beginning of the word *at*.

How can you tell when a vowel has a short sound? One way is to look for two patterns of letters. One short vowel pattern is called the VCC pattern. Words that have this pattern will have one vowel followed by two consonants. These words all have the VCC pattern:

back   send   fist   pond   skunk

A vowel often has a short sound in another pattern. This short vowel pattern is called the VC pattern. Words that have this pattern will have one vowel followed by one consonant at the end of a word. Look at these words. They all have the VC pattern:

bat   ten   sit   pot   tub

Vowels have many sounds. In the next few pages, you will learn the short sounds of vowels. Then you can go on to learn other sounds of vowels.

Short *a*

/a/ back, bat

When the vowel *a* is followed by two consonants, it will probably have the short *a* sound heard in *back*. When *a* is followed by one consonant at the end of a word, it will probably have the short *a* sound heard in *bat*.

Best Guess
for VCC and VC patterns with the vowel *a* = short *a* /a/

Find four words with *a* CC. Say the words.

stack   last   skate   and   brass   tail

Find four words that end with *a* C. Say the words.

Dad   made   flag   plane   pat   has

Now look at each word below. Look at the vowel *a*. Each vowel is followed by either one or two consonants at the end of the word. What sound will each vowel probably have? Read the words.

add	clap	grass	map	track
at	crab	has	past	vast
bath	fast	jazz	rack	vat
Brad	flap	lad	strap	wrap

Read the first two columns of words aloud. Listen for the sound of the short *a*. Which pattern does each word have?

Now read these sentences. Notice the *a*CC or *a*C in the underlined words.

1. I will <u>ask</u> the cook to <u>add</u> a <u>dash</u> of pepper to the soup.

2. The child took a <u>nap</u> on his mother's <u>lap</u>.

3. We will <u>clap</u> for each member of the <u>cast</u> after the <u>last</u> <u>act</u>.

4. I was <u>happy</u> to get a new <u>black</u> <u>hat</u>.

5. The <u>rat</u> slipped through a <u>crack</u> and got away from the <u>cat</u>.

(Extra Practice, p. 169)

— EXCEPTIONS —

See *l*-Controlled Vowels, pp. 72-73. See Letter Team *ar*, pp. 74-75.

Short *e*

/e/ test, bed

When the vowel *e* is followed by two consonants, it will probably have the short *e* sound heard in *test*. When *e* is followed by one consonant at the end of a word, it will probably have the short *e* sound heard in *bed*.

Best Guess
for VCC and VC patterns with the vowel *e* = short *e* /e/

Find four words with *e*CC. Say the words.

best	seem	bend	tell	eat	went

Find four words that end with *e*C. Say the words.

leg	ten	bee	vet	sea	gem

Now look at each word below. Look at the vowel *e*. Each vowel is followed by either one or two consonants at the end of the word. What sound will each vowel probably have? Read the words.

belt	fed	melt	rest	tent
chest	help	met	sell	trend
dent	kept	nest	slept	vent
end	let	pet	speck	web

Read the last column of words aloud. Listen for the sound of the short *e*. Which pattern does each word have?

Now read these sentences. Notice the *e*CC or *e*C in the underlined words.

1. I fed Ben a fried egg.

2. May I use your pen to write the rent check?

3. I'll bet those men like to play chess.

4. My legs felt tired after jogging for ten minutes.

5. Ken went to the crest of the hill to smell the fresh air.

(Extra Practice, p. 169)

— EXCEPTIONS —

See Letter Team *ew*, p. 60.   See Letter Team *er*, pp. 76-77.

Short *i*

/i/ bill, did

When the vowel *i* is followed by two consonants, it will probably have the short *i* sound heard in *bill*. When *i* is followed by one consonant at the end of a word, it will probably have the short *i* sound heard in *did*.

Best Guess
for VCC and VC patterns with the vowel *i* = short *i* /i/

Find four words with *i* CC. Say the words.

ink	mice	twist	trick	mint	dial

Find four words that end with *i*C. Say the words.

whip	sit	lime	dim	pin	ice

Now look at each word below. Look at the vowel *i*. Each vowel is followed by either one or two consonants at the end of the word. What sound will each vowel probably have? Read the words.

big	grim	milk	rib	tip
bit	hint	nip	shrimp	trim
drink	his	pill	strip	twig
fin	kiss	pink	think	zip

Read the words aloud. Listen for the sound of the short *i*. Which pattern does each word have?

Now read these sentences. Notice the *i* CC or *i* C in the underlined words.

1. The cloth may <u>shrink</u> <u>if</u> you <u>dip</u> <u>it</u> <u>in</u> a <u>sink</u> of hot water.

2. <u>His</u> ball must be <u>in</u> the <u>crib</u>.

3. <u>Will</u> <u>Phil</u> <u>rip</u> up the <u>list</u>?

4. When <u>did</u> you <u>slip</u> and <u>hit</u> your <u>shin</u>?

5. During the <u>trip</u>, we hope to <u>fill</u> the <u>ship</u> <u>with</u> <u>fish</u> that we catch.

(Extra Practice, p. 170)

── EXCEPTIONS ──

behind (bi hīnd')   grind (grīnd)   mind (mīnd)
See Letter Teams *igh, ign*, p. 65.   See Letter Team *ir*, p. 78.
See *l*-Controlled Vowels, pp. 72-73.

Short *o*

/o/ dock, top

When the vowel *o* is followed by two consonants, it will probably have the short *o* sound heard in *dock*. When *o* is followed by one consonant at the end of a word, it will probably have the short *o* sound heard in *top*.

Best Guess
for VCC and VC patterns with the vowel *o* = short *o* /o/

Find four words with *o*CC. Say the words.

clock	bond	romp	hole	block	code

Find four words that end with *o*C. Say the words.

hot	got	boil	pop	rob	oat

Now look at each word below. Look at the vowel *o*. Each vowel is followed by either one or two consonants at the end of the word. What sound will each vowel probably have? Read the words.

blond	flock	mob	rock	sob
box	fond	odd	shop	sock
chomp	knock	pot	shot	stomp
crock	lot	prop	slot	trot

Read the words in the first column aloud. Listen for the sound of the short *o*. Which pattern does each word have?

Now read these sentences. Notice the *o*CC or *o*C in the underlined words.

1. <u>Rob</u> <u>got</u> a <u>shock</u> when he fell in the <u>pond</u>.

2. Please <u>stop</u> <u>on</u> the <u>dock</u> to say hello.

3. Did <u>Polly</u> <u>drop</u> the <u>clock</u>?

4. If you <u>hop</u> <u>on</u> <u>top</u> of the <u>cot</u>, it may break.

(Extra Practice, p. 170)

EXCEPTIONS

won (wun)
See Letter Team *ow*, p. 70.
See Vowel *o* with
    Other Consonants, p. 71.

won't (wōnt)
See *l*-Controlled Vowels, pp. 72-73.
See Letter Team *or*, pp. 79-80.

Short *u*

/u/ must, up

When the vowel *u* is followed by two consonants, it will probably have the short *u* sound heard in *must*. When *u* is followed by one consonant at the end of a word, it will probably have the short *u* sound heard in *up*.

Best Guess
for VCC and VC patterns with the vowel *u* = short *u* /u/

Find four words with *u*CC. Say the words.

ruin	rush	bump	duck	tune	rust

Find four words that end with *u*C. Say the words.

fun	Sue	mud	hut	tug	suit

Now look at each word below. Look at the vowel *u*. Each vowel is followed by either one or two consonants at the end of the word. What sound will each vowel probably have? Read the words.

bulb	dumb	hunt	nut	sum
bump	dump	jug	putt	thrust
cub	gun	just	skunk	trust
drug	hum	much	strung	tub

Read the words aloud. Listen for the sound of the short *u*. Which pattern does each word have?

Now read these sentences. Notice the *u*CC or *u*C in the underlined words.

1. Wash the <u>cups</u> in a <u>tub</u> of <u>suds</u> and hot water.

2. <u>Gus</u> <u>dug</u> a hole near the tree <u>stump</u>.

3. A <u>gust</u> of wind sprayed the <u>bus</u> with <u>dust</u>.

4. The baker makes great pie <u>crusts</u> and <u>buns</u>.

(Extra Practice, p. 171)

---EXCEPTIONS---

bull (bŭl)	full (fŭl)	push (pŭsh)
bush (bŭsh)	pull (pŭl)	put (pŭt)

See Letter Team *ur*, pp. 81–82.

Mixed Review: Short Vowels

Practice what you have learned by reading these sentences.

1. Chuck will clip the shrubs next spring.
2. Let's split the bill for the gift.
3. I have a big glass of skim milk.
4. Pam will sew the quilt by hand.
5. He has to have a stick to make a splint for his thumb.
6. I fed the pup and then let it run in the park.
7. Dot got a dress at the thrift shop.
8. How did the cloth get so wet?
9. Tell us when the bus will get to West Acton.
10. Will you lend me your silk scarf?
11. I got this plank at a mill.
12. Jan spent a lot of cash on that red belt.
13. He went to a shop to get a mask.
14. Stick a stamp on the letter.
15. Ted got lost at the bend in the path.
16. Has the cab gone to pick up Fran yet?
17. The judge sat on the bench.
18. Bob sent the plant to Mom.
19. You can cash a check at that bank.
20. He will toss the rock into the pond.
21. Ron has a stiff neck.
22. Bend the twig until it snaps in half.
23. The bell rang to end the class.
24. Fill the trash cans with junk.
25. A skunk can give off a bad scent.

Vowels have many sounds. One common sound that each vowel has is the long vowel sound. The long sound is just like the vowel's name. For example, the long sound of *a* is /ā/, the vowel sound you hear at the beginning of the word *ape*. The long sound of *e* is /ē/, the vowel sound you hear at the end of the word *tree*.

How can you tell when a vowel has a long sound? Look for certain patterns of letters, just as you did for short vowels. One long vowel pattern is called the VCV pattern. Words that have this pattern will have one vowel followed by a consonant and another vowel. The other vowel is often an *e*. For example, these words all have the VCV pattern:

VCV	VCV	VCV	VCV	VCV
take	Steve	bite	home	mule

You should know one other long vowel pattern, the VV(C) pattern. Words with this pattern have two vowels that are teamed together and that are sometimes followed by one consonant. The first vowel in these teams often has a long sound. Here are some words that follow this VV(C) pattern:

VVC	VV	VVC	VVC	VVC
stain	fee	pies	boat	juice

The VVC pattern for long vowels works for many words. However, there are some vowel teams that have whole new sounds. In Part 2, you can learn about those teams.

Long *a*

/ā/ tale, wait

When the vowel *a* is followed by a consonant and then another vowel, it will probably have the long *a* vowel sound heard in *tale*. Usually this VCV pattern for long *a* is *a*C*e*.

When *a* is followed by another vowel and then a consonant, it will probably have the long *a* vowel sound heard in *wait*. Usually this VVC pattern for long *a* is *ai*C .

Best Guess
for VCV and VVC patterns with the vowel *a* = long *a* /ā/

Find four words with *a*C*e* and two words with *ai*C. Say the words.

| ale | fade | skate | plain | waist | trade |

In each of the words below, there is an *a*C*e* or *ai*C pattern. What vowel sound will each word probably have? Read the words.

age	chain	graze	pain	vain
ail	date	jail	plane	vase
braid	fail	mail	stain	wade
cape	gate	male	trail	wail

Listen for the long *a* sound as you read the first column of words aloud.

Now read these sentences. Notice the *a*C*e* or *ai*C in the underlined words.

1. The workers <u>came</u> to <u>pave</u> the road.

2. I <u>aim</u> to <u>bake</u> a <u>cake</u> for <u>Gail</u>.

3. Please put the <u>snails</u> on a <u>plate</u>.

4. The <u>mail</u> <u>came</u> <u>late</u>.

5. The <u>crate</u> was shipped by <u>train</u> to <u>Maine</u>.

(Extra Practice, p. 171)

EXCEPTIONS

aisle (īle)   have (hav)   plaid (plad)   said (sed)

See Letter Team *ar*, pp. 74-75.   See Letter Team *ear*, p. 83.

Long *e*

/ē/ bead, see

When the vowel *e* is followed by another vowel and then a consonant, it will probably have the long *e* vowel sound heard in *bead*. Usually this VVC pattern for long *e* is *ea*C or *ee*C. The long *e* also appears in the VV pattern at the end of a word, as in *see* and *sea*.

Best Guess
for VVC and VV patterns with the vowel *e* = long *e* /ē/

Find four words with *ea*C or *ee*C. Say the words.

| steel | beach | scream | mare | tell | seed |

The vowel *e* appears at the beginning of a VVC or VV pattern in each of the words below. What vowel sound will each word probably have? Read the words.

beet	fee	knee	peace	stream
cheap	feel	leave	screen	tree
cheek	flea	meat	sneak	weed
deal	green	meet	squeeze	yeast

Read the last two columns of words aloud. Listen for the long *e* sound.

Now read these sentences. Notice the VVC and VV patterns in the underlined words.

1. We won three free seats at the concert.

2. Last week, the queen gave a speech.

3. The farmer raises sheep and grows peas and wheat.

4. A deep stream weaves through the valley.

5. The sleek seal lives in the sea.

(Extra Practice, p. 172)

── EXCEPTIONS ──

See Letter Team *ey*, p. 54.
See Letter Team *ea*, pp. 57-58.
See Letter Team *ei*, p. 59.
See Letter Team *eu*, p. 61.

See Letter Team *er*, pp. 76-77.
See Letter Team *ear*, p. 83.
See Letter Teams *air*, *eir*, p. 84.

Long *i*

/ī/ hike, cried, lie

When the vowel *i* is followed by a consonant and then another vowel (VCV pattern), it will probably have the long *i* vowel sound heard in *hike*. Usually the pattern is an *iCe* pattern. The vowel *i* can also have a long sound when it appears in the VVC or VV pattern. Usually the pattern is an *ieC* or an *ie* pattern as in *cried* or *lie*.

Best Guess
for VCV, VVC, and VV patterns with vowel *i* = long *i* /ī/

Find four words with *iCe*. Say the words.

kite   tide   fine   hill   rise   rid

Find four words with *ieC* or *ie*. Say the words.

tie   vie   veil   pie   ice   cried

In each of the words below, there is an *iCe*, *ieC*, or *ie* pattern. What vowel sound will each word probably have? Read the words.

bite	dried	mine	pried	stripe
bride	kite	nice	rice	vine
die	lied	nine	side	wine
dime	like	pile	slide	write

As you read the first column of words aloud, listen for the long *i* sound.

Now read the sentences. Notice the *iCe*, *ieC*, and *ie* patterns in the underlined words.

1. What is the price of this tie?

2. She cried when she won first prize.

3. You may ride your bike if the path has dried.

4. With a sharp knife, dice the chives.

(Extra Practice, p. 172)

EXCEPTIONS

give (giv)
See Letter Team *ia*, p. 62.   See Letter Team *ie*, pp. 63-64.
The word *live* may be pronounced (liv) or (līv).

Long *o*

/ō/ hope, boat, toe

When the vowel *o* is followed by a consonant and then another vowel, it will probably have the long *o* vowel sound heard in *hope*. Usually this VCV pattern for long *o* is *o*C*e*. Often the vowel *o* has a long sound when it appears in a VVC or VV pattern. Usually the pattern is *oa*C or *oe*, as in *boat* or *toe*.

Best Guess
for VCV, VVC, or VV patterns with vowel *o* = long *o* /ō/

Find four words with *o*C*e*. Say the words.

code   close   doll   oil   robe   wrote

Find four words with *oa*C or *oe*. Say the words.

toad   Joe   soap   John   foe   pod

In the words below, there is an *o*C*e*, *oa*C, or *oe* pattern. What sound do you think each *o* will probably have? Read the words.

doe	hole	note	soak	throne
foam	home	oat	stole	tone
goat	joke	pole	stone	woe
hoe	load	road	throat	zone

Read the words aloud. Listen for the long *o* sound.

Now read these sentences. Notice the *o*C*e*, *oa*C, and *oe* patterns in the underlined words.

1. The <u>coach</u> does not <u>smoke</u>.

2. I used the <u>whole</u> <u>loaf</u> of bread.

3. Heat the <u>roast</u> beef on the <u>stove</u>.

4. <u>Joan</u> went <u>home</u> on that <u>road</u> every day.

5. He <u>wrote</u> a <u>note</u> to his friend in <u>Rome</u>.

(Extra Practice, p. 173)

EXCEPTIONS

road (brôd)
ome (kum)
does (duz)
See Letter Teams *oi*, *oy*, p. 66.
See Letter Team *oo*, p. 67.

lose (lüz)
love (luv)
shoe (shü)
See Letter Team *ou*, pp. 68-69.
See Letter Team *or*, pp. 79-80.

some (sum)
whose (hüz)

Long *u*

/ü/ **tune, suit, due**   /yü/ **cute, cue**

When the vowel *u* is followed by a consonant and then another vowel, it will probably have the long *u* sound heard in *tune*. Usually this VCV pattern for long *u* is *u*C*e*. The vowel *u* can also have a long sound when it appears in the VVC or VV pattern. Usually the pattern is *ui*C or *ue*, as in *suit* or *due*. In a few words, this long *u* sound has a *y* sound before it, as heard in *cute* and *cue*.

Best Guess
for VCV, VVC, or VV patterns with vowel *u* = long *u* /ü/ or /yü/

Find four words with *u*C*e* and two words with *ue*. Say the words.

cube   rue   duke   flue   rude   use

The vowel *u* appears in a *u*C*e* or *ue* pattern in each of the words below. What sound will *u* probably have? Read the words.

crude	huge	nude	rule	tube
due	June	plume	spruce	tune
fume	mule	prune	sue	use
fuse	mute	rue	true	yule

Listen for the long *u* sound as you read the words aloud.

Now read these sentences. Notice the *u*C*e*, *ui*C, and *ue* in the underlined words.

1. June likes fruit juice.

2. The glue gives off strong fumes.

3. The blue spruce can grow to be a huge tree.

4. Is it true that the duke is rude?

(Extra Practice, p. 173)

─── EXCEPTIONS ───

build (bild)	guilt (gilt)	suite (swēt)
guide (gīd)	suede (swād)	
See Letter Team *eu*, p. 61.	See Letter Team *ur*, pp. 81-82.	

Mixed Review: Long Vowels

Practice what you have learned by reading these sentences.

1. Joan likes to play tunes on her flute.
2. Wipe the bike with soap and water.
3. What a treat to see a blue spruce tree!
4. Please load the bait into the boat.
5. Place the loam in a crate.
6. Jude will make toast.
7. The oak tree gave a lot of shade.
8. The sheet had a border of lace.
9. The white goat is lame.
10. Let me treat you to a free meal.
11. Let's hike to the stream with Dean.
12. Clean the grime off this stove.
13. That green stone is jade.
14. The queen has quite a lot of pride.
15. He returned to the scene of the crime.
16. As a rule, cats chase mice.
17. Let me drive the blue boat.
18. Is there a phone on this train?
19. I need a tube of white paint.
20. Are whales too huge to be cute?
21. I gave him the clue that solved the case.
22. Smile and wave when the bride walks by.
23. We planted a pine tree in the grove.
24. Sue has a nice green coat.
25. A cruise is quite a nice prize.

More about Vowels

The Schwa Sound

Vowels have three common sounds: a short sound, a long sound, and a special sound called the **schwa** sound. It is the sound you hear at the beginning of the words *about* and *occur*.

Any vowel can stand for the schwa sound. So when words are respelled, a special symbol stands for schwa. This symbol looks like an upside-down *e*, like this: ə.

You can hear the schwa sound anywhere in a word. Sometimes it comes at the beginning of a word, as it does in *about*. Often, though, it comes in the middle or at the end of a word. Say the word *taken*, for example. Can you hear the schwa right before the *n* at the end of the word? The word *circus* has a schwa sound just before the letter *s*.

How can you tell when a vowel has a short sound, a long sound, the schwa sound, or some other sound? Sometimes, this can be hard. The remaining lessons in Part 1 will show you ways to figure this out. However, you will first need to know something about syllables.

Reading Syllables

A **syllable** is a word or word part with one vowel sound. The word *dig*, for example, has one vowel sound and one syllable. The word *digging* has two syllables: *dig* and *ging*. This is often written as dig/ging. Say *digging* to yourself. Can you hear both vowel sounds?

A syllable may have two or more vowels in it, but the vowels will have one sound. For example, say *meeting* (meet/ing) to yourself. The first syllable has two vowels, but they stand for one sound, long *e*. Now say the word *syllable* to yourself. It has three syllables. Can you hear them all?

Reading Long Words

Understanding syllables will help you read well. Many long words can be read one syllable at a time. On the next page are some rules that can help you divide words into syllables.

Try dividing between double letters in the middle of a word:

rabbit = rab / bit   happy = hap / py

Try dividing between two consonants in the middle of a word:

winter = win / ter   perfect = per / fect

If a word has a letter team in the middle, such as *ch* or *ck*, do not divide between those letters. Treat the team as if it were one consonant.

chicken = chick / en   monster = mon / ster

Sometimes a long word is made from two shorter words. Such words are called **compound words**. The words *baseball*, *sunshine*, and *homework* are all compound words. Compound words are usually easy to read once you know they are two words put together.

Many long words are easy to read if you know how. First, look to see if a long word is a compound word. If it isn't, then look for special letter patterns in the word. The remaining lessons in Part 1 will tell you what to look for.

Short *a* in Words with Two or More Syllables

/a/ racket

When the vowel *a* is followed by two consonants (VCC pattern), it will probably have the short *a* sound heard in *racket*. This same short vowel pattern applies to one-syllable words.

Best Guess
for VCC patterns with the vowel *a* = short *a* /a/

Find four words with *a*CC. Say the words.

happy   rainy   packet   captive   basic   drastic

Now look at each of the words below. In each word, the vowel *a* appears in the *a*CC pattern. What sound will each *a* probably have? Read the words.

annex	captive	gallop	matter	sample
apple	dazzle	handicap	paddle	scamper
baffle	fabric	lantern	pamper	tantrum
bracket	fantastic	master	random	wrathful

Read the words aloud. Listen for the short *a* sound in each word.

Now read these sentences. Notice the *a*CC in the underlined words.

1. <u>After</u> you ride the horse, put the <u>saddle</u> in the shed.

2. <u>Patty</u> put <u>candles</u> on the <u>mantle</u>.

3. Take the <u>wrapper</u> off the bag of <u>plastic</u> spoons.

4. Please put this dirty <u>jacket</u> in the <u>hamper</u>.

5. The <u>actor</u> wore a <u>flannel</u> shirt.

(Extra Practice, p. 174)

EXCEPTIONS

aching (āk'ing)
danger (dān'jər)
See Letter Team *aw*, p. 56.

father (fä'ŦHər)
stranger (strān'jər)
See Letter Team *ar*, pp. 74-75.

Short *e* in Words with Two or More Syllables

/e/ dentist

When the vowel *e* is followed by two consonants (VCC pattern), it will probably have the short *e* sound heard in *dentist*. This same short vowel pattern applies to one-syllable words.

Best Guess
for VCC patterns with the vowel *e* = short *e* /e/

Find four words with *e*CC. Say the words.

gender   selfish   beastly   lesson   legal   Wendy

Now look at each of the words below. Find the vowel *e* in the *e*CC pattern. What sound will each *e* probably have? Read the words.

beckon	frenzy	Jenny	pepper	stencil
cellophane	gremlin	kettle	pretzel	temperament
Edward	hemlock	Kremlin	remnant	tender
emblem	injected	lesson	septic	yellow

Read the words aloud. Listen for the short *e* sound in each word.

Now read these sentences. Notice the *e*CC in the underlined words.

. Say <u>hello</u> when you pass through <u>Denver</u>.

. The <u>members</u> of the cast are <u>resting</u> now.

. <u>Benny</u> added <u>pepper</u> to the stew.

. Do you know <u>whether</u> he got the <u>fender</u> fixed?

. I wouldn't <u>invest</u> more than a <u>penny</u> in that <u>venture</u>!

(Extra Practice, p. 174)

EXCEPTIONS

See Letter Team *ew*, p. 60.   See Letter Team *er*, pp. 76-77.

Short *i* in Words with Two or More Syllables

/i/ silver

When the vowel *i* is followed by two consonants (VCC pattern), it will probably have the short *i* sound heard in *silver*. This same short vowel pattern applies to one-syllable words.

Best Guess
for VCC patterns with the vowel *i* = short *i* /i/

Find four words with *i*CC. Say the words.

Richard	timeless	dinner	pistol	sister	reside

Now look at the vowel *i* in each of the words below. In each word, *i* appears in the *i*CC pattern. What sound will each *i* probably have? Read the words.

bitterly	dizzy	himself	mistake	risky
blister	fidget	inland	mitten	victim
dimmer	fifteen	kicker	nickel	vindictive
distant	grimmest	kidnap	picnicking	window

Read the words aloud. Listen for the short *i* sound in each word.

Now read the sentences. Notice the *i*CC in the underlined words.

1. <u>Billy</u> was a <u>witness</u> to the crime.

2. The <u>swimmer</u> was <u>brimming</u> with energy.

3. The <u>kicker</u> could not <u>dismiss</u> the <u>wisdom</u> of the coach's advice.

4. Some <u>insects</u> are more than two <u>inches</u> long.

5. The <u>shipper</u> lost the carton of <u>dishes</u>.

(Extra Practice, p. 175)

EXCEPTIONS

island (ī'lend)
See Letter Teams *igh*, *ign*, p. 65.   See Letter Team *ir*, p. 78.

Short *o* in Words with Two or More Syllables

/o/ pocket

When the vowel *o* is followed by two consonants (VCC pattern), it will probably have the short *o* sound heard in *pocket*. This same short vowel pattern applies to one-syllable words.

Best Guess

for VCC patterns with the vowel *o* = short *o* /o/

Find four words with *o*CC. Say the words.

cosmic　　goblet　　robber　　hopeful　　coaster　　locket

Look at the vowel *o* in each of the words below. The *o* appears in the *o*CC pattern in each word. What sound will the *o* probably have? Read the words.

bonnet	fondly	monster	problematic	somber
copper	goblin	nonsense	respond	sonnet
cosmic	hockey	oddity	rocket	wobble
droplet	hostility	ponder	roster	yonder

Read the words aloud. Listen for the short *o* sound in each word.

Now read these sentences. Notice the *o*CC in the underlined words.

1. Please don't <u>bother</u> Mr. <u>Potter</u> while he's sleeping.
2. <u>Holly</u> has made great <u>progress</u> on her big <u>project</u>.
3. Will these <u>objects</u> fit in your <u>locker</u>?
4. Would you like some <u>popcorn</u>, <u>Polly</u>?
5. The <u>sponsor</u> asked for a signed copy of the <u>contract</u>.

(Extra Practice, p. 175)

——EXCEPTIONS——

brother (bruŦH'ər)　　　　other (uŦH'ər)　　wonder (wun'dər)
mother (muŦH'ər)　　　　poster(pō'stər)

See Letter Team *ow*, p. 70.　　See Letter Team *or*, pp. 79-80.
See *l*-Controlled Vowels, pp. 72-73.

Short *u* in Words with Two or More Syllables

/u/ number

When the vowel *u* is followed by two consonants (VCC pattern), it will probably have the short *u* sound heard in *number*. This same short vowel pattern applies to one-syllable words.

Best Guess
for VCC patterns with the vowel *u* = short *u* /u/

Find four words with *u*CC. Say the words.

drummer   gusto   lumber   pruning   usher   housing

Now look at each of the words below. Look at the vowel *u* in the *u*CC pattern. What sound will each *u* probably have? Read the words.

abundant	conducted	humble	nugget	slumber
bluster	druggist	husband	plummet	summit
bundle	dungaree	inducted	pungent	tunnel
chunky	funnel	injustice	rumpus	vulgar

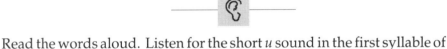

Read the words aloud. Listen for the short *u* sound in the first syllable of each word.

Now read these sentences. Notice the *u*CC in the underlined words.

1. That dress has <u>stunning</u> <u>buttons</u> on it.

2. The <u>subject</u> of sources of <u>funding</u> came up at the meeting.

3. <u>Summer</u> is filled with <u>sunny</u> days.

4. The <u>plumber</u> is <u>flushing</u> out the pipes.

5. For <u>supper</u>, we'll have roast turkey with <u>stuffing</u>.

(Extra Practice, p. 176)

--- EXCEPTIONS ---

bullet (bŭl'it)   pulley (pŭl'ē)
See Letter Team *ur*, pp. 81-82.

Long *a* in Words with Two or More Syllables

/ā/ sailor, bacon

When the vowel *a* is followed by another vowel and then a consonant (VVC pattern), it will probably have the long *a* sound heard in *sailor*. Usually this pattern for long *a* is *ai*C.

When the vowel *a* is followed by a consonant and a vowel (VCV pattern), the *a* will probably have the long *a* sound heard in *bacon*.

Best Guess
for VVC and VCV patterns with the vowel *a* = long *a* /ā/

Find two words with *ai*C and two words with *a*CV. Say the words.

| daisy | grateful | taller | waiting | nation | scamper |

Now look at each of the words below. In each word the vowel *a* appears in the VVC or the VCV pattern. What sound will each *a* probably have? Read the words.

afraid	brazen	failure	hated	raisin
aimless	contagious	faithfully	labor	spacecraft
basin	crater	famous	ovation	traitor
blatantly	evade	graceful	paisley	whaler

Read the words aloud. Listen for the /ā/ sound in each word.

Read these sentences. Notice the *ai*C or *a*CV in the underlined words.

1. <u>Dana</u>, will you do me a <u>favor</u>?

2. I'm <u>grateful</u> that it's not <u>raining</u>.

3. The <u>painter</u> is using <u>latex</u> paint on the <u>railing</u>.

4. The <u>Raiders</u> are <u>claiming</u> a victory.

5. The <u>trainer</u> is <u>taming</u> the lion.

(Extra Practice, p. 176)

EXCEPTIONS

water (wô'tər)
See Second Best Guess for VCV, pp. 43-44.
See Letter Team *ar*, pp. 74-75.   See Letter Teams *air*, *eir*, p. 84.

Long *e* in Words with Two or More Syllables

/ē/ seeing, beater, meter

When the vowel *e* is followed by another vowel at the end of a syllable (VV pattern), it will probably have the long *e* sound heard in *seeing*. When *e* is followed by another vowel and then a consonant (VVC pattern), it will probably have the long vowel sound heard in *beater*. When *e* is followed by a consonant and a vowel (VCV pattern), the *e* will probably have the long vowel sound heard in *meter*.

Best Guess
for VV, VVC, and VCV patterns with the vowel *e* = long *e* /ē/

Find four words that have *e*V at the end of a syllable, *e*VC, or *e*CV.

cheaper　　legal　　　season　　　yellow　　　cheerful　　　better

Now look at the vowel *e* in each of the words below. In each word, *e* appears in the VV, VVC, or VCV pattern. What sound will each *e* probably have? Read the words.

agreement	creepy	fever	peering	seamstress
breezy	equal	geezer	penal	seething
ceiling	evil	heathen	proceeding	sequel
convene	feedback	illegal	really	sequin

Read the words aloud. Listen for the /ē/ sound in each word.

Read these sentences. Notice the *e*V at the end of a syllable, the *e*VC, or the *e*CV in the underlined words.

1. Steven is a dreamer.

2. By reaching the border, they gained their freedom.

3. My teenaged son is cleaning his room.

4. The team holds weekly meetings.

(Extra Practice, p. 177)

— EXCEPTIONS —

See Second Best Guess for VCV, pp. 43-44.
See Letter Team *ea*, pp. 57-58.　　　See Letter Team *ear*, p. 83.
See Letter Team *ei*, p. 59.　　　　　See Letter Teams *air*, *eir*, p. 84.
See Letter Team *er*, pp. 76-77.　　　See Letter Team *ier*, p. 85.

Long *i* in Words with Two or More Syllables
/ī/ fiber

When the vowel *i* is followed by a consonant and a vowel (VCV pattern), it will probably have the long *i* sound heard in *fiber*.

Best Guess
for VCV pattern with the vowel *i* = long i /ī/

Find four words with *i*CV. Say the words.

rider	silly	driving	idol	picking	likely

Now look at each of these two-syllable words. Look at the vowel *i* as it appears in the *i*CV pattern. What sound will *i* probably have? Read the words.

abide	entice	icy	ninety	recital
biting	excitement	lifeless	pirate	siding
bridal	final	liner	primary	tidy
crisis	grimy	minor	privately	visor

Read the words aloud and listen for the /ī/ sound in each one.

Read the sentences. Notice the VCV pattern in the underlined words.

1. <u>Dinah</u> is <u>writing</u> a paper about the <u>Vikings</u>.
2. It was a <u>surprise</u> to see how <u>precise</u> the weave of the <u>fiber</u> could be.
3. On <u>Friday</u>, we'll be <u>dining</u> with friends.
4. The <u>timer</u> sat on the <u>sidelines</u> during the game.
5. Sam <u>resides</u> in a <u>tiny</u> <u>mining</u> town.

(Extra Practice, p. 177)

---EXCEPTIONS---

See Second Best Guess for VCV, pp. 43-44.
See Letter Team *ie*, pp. 63-64.

Long *o* in Words with Two or More Syllables

/o/ boating, bonus

When the vowel *o* is followed by another vowel and then a consonant (VVC pattern), it will probably have the long vowel sound heard in *boating*. Usually this pattern for long *o* is *oa*C. When the vowel *o* is followed by a consonant and another vowel (VCV pattern), the *o* will most likely have the long vowel sound heard in *bonus*.

Best Guess
for VVC and VCV patterns with the vowel *o* = long *o* /ō/

Find two words with *oa*C and two words with *o*CV. Say the words.

spoken   moment   oaken   Johnny   coating   dollar

Now look at each of the words in the list below. Look at the vowel *o*. In each word, *o* appears in the VVC or VCV pattern. What sound will each *o* probably have? Read the words.

bonus	dosage	fomenting	joker	potent
broken	envelope	gloating	locate	rodent
croaking	foamy	homely	noted	toasted
devote	focus	impose	odor	vocalize

Read the words aloud. Can you hear the /ō/ sound in each word?

Read these sentences. Notice the *oa* C or *o* CV pattern in the underlined words.

1. Rosie plays goalie on the soccer team.

2. The homesick child was lonely.

3. George coasted down the hill on his motorcycle.

4. The toaster was stolen.

5. I've chosen oatmeal for breakfast.

(Extra Practice, p. 178)

EXCEPTIONS

closet (kloz'it)

See Second Best Guess for VCV, pp. 43-44.

See Letter Teams *oi, oy*, p. 66.

See Letter Team *oo*, p. 67.

See Letter Team *ou*, pp. 68-69.

See Letter Team *ow*, p. 70.

See Vowel *o* with Other Consonants, p. 71.

See Letter Team *or*, pp. 79-80.

Long *u* in Words with Two or More Syllables

/ü/ suitor, cruel, prudent   /yü/ music

When the vowel *u* is followed by another vowel and then a consonant (VVC pattern), it will probably have the long *u* sound heard in *suitor*. In some words, the letter team *ue* will form parts of different syllables, as in *cruel*. When the vowel *u* is followed by a consonant and a vowel (VCV pattern), the *u* will probably have the long vowel sound heard in *prudent*. In a few words, the long *u* sound has a *y* sound before it, as in *music*.

Best Guess
for VVC and VCV patterns with the vowel *u* = long *u* /ü/ or /yü/

Find three words that have either the VVC or VCV pattern. Say the words.

| lucid | putty | grueling | nuisance | sunny |

Now look at the words below. In each word, *u* appears in the VVC or VCV pattern. What sound will each *u* probably have? Read the words.

argument	fuel	immune	numeral	rescue
butane	glucose	include	produce	truest
cutest	hugest	mucus	prudent	tunic
fluent	humid	mutate	pursue	universe

Read the words aloud and listen for the long *u* sound in each word.

Read these sentences. Notice the VVC or VCV pattern in the underlined words.

1. A stubborn <u>human</u> being is sometimes called <u>mulish</u>.

2. The <u>students</u> went to <u>Munich</u>.

3. Water is a very <u>useful</u> <u>fluid</u>.

4. My <u>tutor</u> <u>uses</u> the blackboard to show examples.

5. We've been on many <u>super</u> <u>cruises</u>.

(Extra Practice, p. 178)

--- EXCEPTIONS ---

busy (biz′ē)   sugar (shŭg′ər)
See Second Best Guess for VCV, pp. 43-44.
See Letter Team *ur*, pp. 81-82.

Second Best Guess for VCV

/a/ cabin   **/e/** metal   **/i/** vivid   **/o/** comic   **/u/** punish

The VCV pattern is a difficult pattern. In the long vowel lessons, you learn that the Best Guess for the VCV pattern is the long vowel. However, in many words with more than one syllable, the first vowel in the VCV pattern has a short vowel sound. You will need to try both the Best Guess and the second best guess in words with more than one syllable and a VCV pattern. Say the words until you hear a word you recognize.

Best Guess
for VCV pattern in two-syllable words = long vowel
Second best guess = short vowel

Look at the words below. They all have the VCV pattern with a short vowel.

banish	damage	honor	panic	shiver
buxom	denim	lemon	punish	study
cavern	figure	linen	relic	toxic
closet	granite	lizard	satin	tribute
credit	hazard	modern	second	volume

Read the words aloud. Listen for the short vowel sound in the first syllable of each word.

Now look at the lists below. The words all have the VCV pattern with a long vowel.

ego	future	liven	ozone	sober
even	hobo	major	poker	tiger
evil	human	miner	razor	total
fatal	idol	mutual	rumor	vapor
funeral	legal	native	slimy	zenith

Read the words aloud. Listen for the long vowel sound in the first syllable of each word.

Read the sentences on the next page.

Now read these sentences. Find the VCV pattern in each word. Try the Best Guess first. If you do not hear a word you recognize, try the second best guess.

1. A high <u>fever</u> can <u>make</u> you <u>shiver</u>.

2. They were <u>fined</u> for <u>polluting</u> the <u>river</u> with <u>toxic</u> waste.

3. The <u>linen</u> <u>blazer</u> costs more than the <u>denim</u> jacket.

4. I've <u>never</u> been in such a <u>huge</u> <u>hotel</u>.

5. The <u>mason</u> <u>used</u> a <u>level</u> to see if the wall was straight.

(Extra Practice, p. 179)

Schwa

/ə/ ago wagon

You have learned that vowels can have either a short sound or a long sound. Vowels can have a third sound, too. It is called the **schwa** sound. In dictionary respellings it looks like an upside down *e*, or /ə/.

In every word of two or more syllables, one syllable is stressed. It gets more emphasis than other syllables in the word. The word *ago* breaks into syllables like this: a/go. The second syllable, which contains the long *o* sound, is stressed. The first syllable is not stressed. The vowel sound in the first syllable of *ago* is the schwa sound. The schwa sound appears only in unstressed syllables.

Each of the five vowels can have the same schwa sound. It is the sound that the vowel *a* has at the beginning of *ago*. It is the sound that the vowel *o* has at the end of *wagon*.

Best Guess
for vowels in unstressed syllables = schwa sound /ə/

Tell which vowel stands for the schwa sound in each of these words.

listed	royal	button	pencil	circus

Now read the two-syllable words below. Listen for the schwa sound in the unstressed syllable.

alive	carrot	gospel	patrol	talent
aspen	China	hopeful	pencil	wishful
campus	fragrant	human	propose	zebra

Read the words aloud. Listen for the schwa sound in each one.

Now read these sentences. Notice the schwa sound in the underlined words.

1. The <u>children</u> <u>agreed</u> to wear their wool <u>sweaters</u>.

2. We rode in a <u>canoe</u> to the <u>cabin</u>.

3. The <u>camels</u> marched <u>along</u> in the <u>circus</u> <u>parade</u>.

4. <u>Donna</u> likes to eat <u>melon</u>.

5. What is the best <u>method</u> for making <u>muffins</u>?

(Extra Practice, p. 179)

Vowel *y*

/ī/ sky, apply, style   /ē/ tricky   /i/ gym

The letter *y* can be either a consonant or a vowel. When it is a consonant, it usually comes at the beginning of a word and stands for the /y/ sound heard in *yes* and *yard*.

When *y* is a vowel, it usually comes in the middle or at the end of a word. You can tell that it is a vowel because it appears in a syllable that contains no other vowels. As a vowel, *y* can stand for the long *i* sound, the long *e* sound, or the short *i* sound. The letter *y* can also be part of letter teams, as you can see in Part 2.

When *y* appears at the end of a one-syllable word, it usually stands for the long *i* sound heard in *sky*. When *y* appears as the vowel in the last syllable of a word that has two or more syllables, it usually has the long *e* sound heard in *tricky*. In some words of two or more syllables, the vowel *y* may have the long *i* sound heard in *apply*.

Best Guess
for *y* at the end of a one-syllable word = long *i* /ī/
for *y* at the end of a two-or-more-syllable word = long *e* /ē/
Second best guess for *y* at the end of a two-or-more-syllable word = long *i* /ī/

Find four words in which the vowel *y* has the long *i* sound. Where does the *y* appear? Say the words. How many syllables are in each word? Are any other vowels in the syllables?

dry	yard	my	pay	sly	spy

Look at the words below. How many syllables are in each word? What sound will each *y* probably have? Read the words. Try the Best Guess first. If you don't recognize a word, try the second best guess.

lady	reply	only	lullaby	hefty	funny

Find the vowel *y* in each word in the list below. How many syllables does each word have? Read the words. Try the Best Guess first. If you don't recognize a word, try the second best guess.

angry	defy	imply	reply	story
beautify	dirty	marry	risky	tidy
by	fly	melody	satisfy	very
classify	fry	memory	shy	why
cry	hungry	rainy	spry	wry

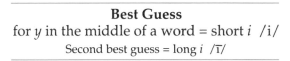

Read the words aloud. Listen for the sound of *y* in each word.

Now read these sentences. Notice the sound of *y* in the underlined words.

1. If you are <u>hungry</u>, <u>try</u> some of the beef stew.

2. <u>Kathy</u> will <u>fly</u> to New York <u>City</u> next week.

3. <u>Why</u> don't you <u>apply</u> for a job at this <u>company</u>?

4. <u>Thirty</u> people came to <u>my</u> surprise <u>party</u>.

5. I can't <u>deny</u> that I have been <u>lucky</u> <u>lately</u>.

(Extra Practice, p. 180)

When *y* appears as a vowel in the middle of a word containing one or more syllables, it usually has the /i/ sound heard in gym. In some words in which *y* appears in the middle, the vowel *y* may have the /ī/ sound heard in the word *style*.

Best Guess
for *y* in the middle of a word = short *i* /i/
Second best guess = long *i* /ī/

Find the words in which *y* appears as a vowel in the middle of the word. Say the words. Listen for the short *i* or long *i* sound.

system	yonder	type	flying	carry	hymn

Now look at each word in the list on the next page.

The vowel *y* appears in the middle of each word in the list below. What sound will each *y* probably have? Try the Best Guess first. Listen and use your common sense. If you don't recognize a word, try the second best guess.

abyss	dryer	myself	rhyme	symbol
acrylic	dynamite	mystic	rhythm	typical
bicycle	gymnasium	nylon	rye	typist
cylinder	hypnotist	oxygen	syllable	tyrant

Read the words aloud. Can you hear the sound of *y* in each word?

Now read these sentences. Notice the sound of *y* in the underlined words.

1. The hair stylist dyed my hair black.

2. Nylon is a synthetic material.

3. He said goodbye and got onto his motorcycle.

4. I forced myself to go to the gym to work out.

5. Cynthia works as a typist.

(Extra Practice, p. 180)

Mixed Review

Practice what you have learned by reading these sentences.

1. I was trying to save every penny.
2. Donald was reading the paper.
3. For safety, use plastic cups when you go hiking.
4. The bridal party included Susan's parents.
5. The staff members were given a bonus.
6. Her reply was that the story was nonsense.
7. The taste of the lemon may linger in your mouth.
8. I found Kathy's wedding dress in the old suitcase.
9. Our family rented a small boat for the trip down the river.
10. We rested for forty minutes.
11. The circus band has chosen exciting music.
12. This is the second time I have broken my glasses.
13. Last summer we traveled to Munich.
14. My husband is hopeful that Jenny will visit.
15. Don't bother to finish the project today.
16. The basin was filled with soapy water.
17. Danny was frying some bacon.
18. I have never driven to the city of Akron.
19. The tailor fixed the suit very quickly.
20. He was making some progress on his studies.
21. Roger was selling hot pretzels at the roadside.
22. What method did Ellen use to bring Donald to his senses?
23. The meter maid left a ticket on my truck.
24. Let's go fishing in the country next summer.
25. Benny was planning a party for Richard.

PART 2 · LETTER TEAMS

Letter teams are groups of letters that you see together in many words. A letter team may be a pair of vowels, such as *ee* or *ai*. A letter team may be a group of consonants, such as *spl*. Some letter teams have consonants and vowels in them, as in *squ* or *aw*.

Letter teams can be tricky. When letters team together, the team may have a sound you do not expect. For instance, the words *write* and *right* sound the same, but each word has different letters in it. In *write*, the letter team *wr* stands for the /r/ sound and the letter *i* stands for the long *i* sound. In *right*, the letter *r* stands for the /r/ sound and the letter team *igh* stands for long *i*. If you do not know the letter teams *wr* and *igh*, you may not be able to read the words *write* and *right*.

Certain vowel teams are covered in Part 1. Part 2 of this book will teach you many other letter teams. See how many letter teams you already know. The key words below and on the next page have the letter teams from Part 2.

pay	/ā/	page 53		**thief**	/ē/	page 63
key	/ē/	page 54		**pie**	/ī/	page 63
they	/ā/	page 54		**diet**	/ī'ə/	page 63
cause	/ô/	page 55		**light**	/ī/	page 65
law	/ô/	page 56		**sign**	/ī/	page 65
bead	/ē/	page 57		**boil**	/oi/	page 66
head	/e/	page 57		**boy**	/oi/	page 66
great	/ā/	page 57		**school**	/ü/	page 67
vein	/ā/	page 59		**book**	/u̇/	page 67
seize	/ē/	page 59		**out**	/ou/	page 68
chew	/ü/	page 60		**young**	/u/	page 68
few	/yü/	page 60		**cow**	/ou/	page 70
neutral	/ü/	page 61		**snow**	/ō/	page 70
feud	/yü/	page 61		**off**	/ô/	page 71
media	/ē'ə/	page 62		**talk**	/ô/	page 72
dial	/ī'ə/	page 62		**wild**	/ī/	page 72

old	/ō/	page 72	favor	/ər/	page 79
car	/är/	page 74	word	/ėr/	page 79
care	/er/	page 74	fur	/ėr/	page 81
carry	/ar/	page 74	jury	/ùr/	page 81
dollar	/ər/	page 74	pure	/yür/	page 81
war	/ôr/	page 74	picture	/ər/	page 81
term	/ėr/	page 76	ear	/ir/	page 83
very	/er/	page 76	learn	/ėr/	page 83
after	/ər/	page 76	bear	/er/	page 83
here	/ir/	page 76	hair	/er/	page 84
bird	/ėr/	page 78	their	/er/	page 84
fire	/īr/	page 78	happier	/ē'ər/	page 85
for	/ôr/	page 79	flier	/ī'ər/	page 85
sorry	/or/	page 79	pier	/ir/	page 85

Letter Team *ay*

/ā/ pay

The *ay* letter team will probably have the long *a* sound heard in *pay*.

Best Guess
for *ay* = long *a* /ā/

Find four words that contain the letter team *ay*. Say the words.

play   many   relay   Sally   away   spray

Now look at the words below. Each word contains the letter team *ay*. What vowel sound will *ay* probably stand for in each word? Read the words.

bay	day	laying	pray	stay
betray	decay	maybe	Raymond	stray
bluejay	essay	playing	rayon	Sunday
clay	hay	portray	runway	wayside

Read the words aloud. Listen for the sound of the long *a* in each word.

Read these sentences. Notice the long *a* sound in the underlined words.

1. On <u>Tuesday</u> morning, <u>Wayne</u> took the <u>subway</u> to work.

2. In <u>May</u>, I made the final <u>payment</u> on my car loan.

3. It will <u>dismay</u> me if you <u>say</u> that you can't come for dinner.

4. <u>Kay's</u> hair is turning <u>gray.</u>

5. I'm afraid your <u>paycheck</u> will be <u>delayed</u> this week.

(Extra Practice, p. 180)

— EXCEPTION —

says (sez)

Letter Team *ey*

/ē/ key   /ā/ they

The *ey* letter team will probably have the long *e* sound heard in *key*. In some words, the *ey* letter team has the long *a* sound heard in *they*.

Best Guess
for *ey* = long *e* /ē/
Second best guess = long *a* /ā/

Find four words that contain the *ey* letter team. Say the words. Notice what letters stand for the long *e* or the long *a* sound in each word.

turkey   testy   very   prey   obey   money

Now look at the words below. Each word contains the letter team *ey*. What vowel sound will *ey* probably stand for in each word? Try the Best Guess first. If you don't recognize a word, try the second best guess. Read the words.

alley	hockey	keyhole	paisley	valley
chimney	honey	monkey	parsley	volley
convey	jersey	New Jersey	pulley	volleyball
donkey	jockey	obey	surveyor	disobey

Read the words aloud. Listen for the sound of the long *e* or the long *a* in each one.

Read these sentences. Notice the long *e* or long *a* sound in the underlined words.

1. The city took a <u>survey</u> to find out the feelings of <u>trolley</u> riders.

2. It may cost a lot of <u>money</u> to get the <u>chimney</u> fixed.

3. <u>Harvey</u> likes to play <u>volleyball</u>.

4. The stubborn <u>donkey</u> often <u>disobeyed</u> its owner.

5. The <u>hockey</u> team members got their new <u>jerseys</u>.

(Extra Practice, p. 181)

--- EXCEPTION ---

eye (ī)

Letter Team *au*

/ô/ cause

The *au* letter team will probably have the /ô/ sound heard in *cause*.

Best Guess
for *au* = /ô/ cause

Find four words that contain the letter team *au*. Say the words. Notice the /ô/ sound in each word.

Paul	salute	fault	August	dual	laundry

Now look at the words below. Each word contains the letter team *au*. What vowel sound will *au* probably stand for in each word? Read the words.

auburn	caustic	fraud	launch	sauce
author	daughter	haughty	laundry	slaughter
auto	faucet	haul	naughty	taught
caught	fault	hydraulic	restaurant	vault

Read the words aloud. Listen for the /ô/ sound heard in *cause*.

Read these sentences. Notice the sound that the letter team *au* has in the underlined words.

1. Laurence is writing a report about James Audubon.
2. My daughter wants to be an author.
3. After a short pause, the audience began clapping.
4. Launder the gauze slip in cold water.
5. The vault has an automatic lock.

(Extra Practice, p. 181)

--- EXCEPTIONS ---

aunt (ant) or (änt)	gauge (gāj)	laugh (laf)	mauve (mōv)

Letter Team *aw*

/ô/ law

The *aw* letter team will probably have the /ô/ sound heard in *law*. This sound is the same sound the *au* stands for in *cause*.

Best Guess
for *aw* = /ô/ law

Find four words that contain the letter team *aw*. Say the words. Notice the /ô/ sound in each word.

whale   crawl   hawk   wake   yawn   draw

Now look at the words below. Each word contains the letter team *aw*. What vowel sound will *aw* probably stand for in each word? Read the words.

brawl	fawn	paw	saw	squawk
dawn	flaw	pawn	scrawl	straw
claw	lawn	prawn	scrawny	thaw
drawn	lawyer	raw	shawl	yawning

Read the words aloud. Listen for the /ô/ sound heard in *law*.

Read these sentences. Notice the sound that the letter team *aw* has in the underlined words.

1. <u>Dawn</u> made cole <u>slaw</u> for the picnic.

2. He <u>saw</u> a <u>lawn</u> mower that he wanted to buy.

3. The jewel is not expensive because it has an <u>awful</u> <u>flaw</u>.

4. They <u>sprawled</u> on the <u>lawn</u> chairs under the <u>awning</u>.

5. The power of the <u>hawk</u> was <u>awesome</u>.

(Extra Practice, p. 182)

Letter Team *ea*

/ē/ **bead**   /e/ **head**   /ā/ **great**

The *ea* letter team will probably have the long *e* sound heard in *bead*. In many words, however, the *ea* letter team has the short *e* sound heard in *head*. In a few words, the *ea* letter team stands for the long *a* sound heard in *great*.

Best Guess
for *ea* = long *e* /ē/
Second best guess = short e /e/
Third best guess = long *a* /ā/

Find four words in which the letter team *ea* stands for the long *e* sound. Say the words.

meat   stake   ahead   please   dream   season

Find four words below in which the letter team *ea* stands for the short *e* sound. Say the words. What sound do the letters *ea* stand for in the other two words?

death   ready   break   bread   heaven   steak

Now look at the words below. Each word contains the letter team *ea*. What vowel sound will *ea* probably stand for in each word? Try the Best Guess first. If you don't recognize some words, try the second and third best guesses. Read the words.

beaches	feast	heavy	measles	steak
beaver	feather	jealous	measure	stream
break	grease	leader	pleasing	sneakers
dread	greatest	meadow	pleasant	treat

Read the words aloud. Listen for the sound of long *e*, short *e*, or long *a* in each word.

Now read the sentences on the next page.

Read these sentences. Notice the long *e*, short *e*, or long *a* sound in the underlined words.

1. We had <u>wheatcakes</u> for <u>breakfast</u>.

2. I was <u>eager</u> to <u>read</u> the <u>weather</u> report.

3. It's a <u>great</u> day to go to the <u>beach</u>.

4. Hamburger is <u>cheaper</u> than <u>steak</u> or <u>seafood</u>.

5. I bought a <u>leather</u> <u>leash</u> for my <u>beagle</u>.

(Extra Practice, p. 182)

EXCEPTIONS

See Letter Team *ear*, p. 83.
The word *lead* may be pronounced (lēd) or (led).
The word *read* may be pronounced (rēd) or (red).

Letter Team *ei*

/ā/ vein   /ē/ seize

When the letter team *ei* is followed by *g* or *n*, the *ei* will probably have the long *a* sound heard in *vein*. When the letter team *ei* is followed by any letter other than *g* or *n* in a word or syllable, it will probably have the long *e* sound heard in *seize*.

Best Guess
for *ei* = long *e* /ē/
for *ei* followed by *g* or *n* = long *a* /ā/

Find four words in which the letter team *ei* is followed by *g* or *n*. Say the words.

eight	weird	vein	reign	design	weigh

Now look at the words below. Each word contains the letter team *ei*. What letter follows the letter team *ei*? What does that letter tell you about which vowel sound *ei* will stand for in each word? Read the words.

beige	eighteen	leisure	receipt	sleigh
deceive	eighth	neighbor	receive	weight
deign	freight	rein	seizure	weird

Listen for the sound of the long *a* or the long *e* as you read the words aloud.

Read these sentences. Notice the long *a* or long *e* sound in the under-lined words.

1. We rode in a <u>sleigh</u> pulled by <u>reindeer</u>.

2. The dog <u>weighed</u> <u>eighty</u> pounds.

3. She bought a <u>skein</u> of <u>beige</u> yarn.

4. You will <u>receive</u> a <u>receipt</u> in the mail.

5. The truck driver had to have the <u>freight</u> <u>weighed</u>.

(Extra Practice, p. 183)

─── EXCEPTIONS ───

height (hīt)   veil (vāl)   See Letter Teams *air*, *eir*, p. 84.

Letter Team *ew*

/ü/ chew   /yü/ few

The *ew* letter team will probably have the /ü/ sound heard in *chew* or the /yü/ sound heard in *few*. These sounds are the same vowel sounds heard in *tune* and *cute*.

Best Guess
for *ew* = long *u* /ü/ or /yü/

Find four words that contain the letter team *ew*. Say the words. Notice the /ü/ or /yü/ sound in each word.

brew   wed   view   skewer   stew   wet

Now look at the words below. Each word contains the letter team *ew*. What vowel sound will *ew* probably stand for in each one? Read the words.

anew	dew	jewel	pewter	stewardess
blew	drew	Jewish	screw	strew
cashew	flew	knew	shrew	threw
crew	grew	new	slew	yew

Read the words aloud. Listen for the sound of /ü/ or /yü/ in each word.

Read these sentences. Notice the sound that the letter team *ew* has in the underlined words.

1. The jeweler made a new setting for my ring.

2. The stewardess took coffee to the other crew members.

3. A large bird flew into view.

4. Drew is a shrewd businessman.

5. The wind blew a few clothes off the clothesline.

(Extra Practice, p. 183)

--- EXCEPTION ---

sew (sō)

Letter Team *eu*
/ü/ neutral   /yü/ feud

The *eu* letter team will probably have the /ü/ vowel sound heard in *neutral* or the /yü/ sound heard in *feud*. These sounds are the same vowel sounds heard in *tune* and *cute*.

Best Guess
for *eu* = long *u* /ü/ or /yü/

Find two words that contain the letter team *eu*. Say the words. Notice the /ü/ or /yü/ sound in each word.

Eugene   elude   sleuth   prune

Now look at the words below. Each word contains the letter team *eu*. What vowel sound will *eu* probably stand for in each word? Read the words.

deuce	eulogy	neuter	neutron	rheumatism
eucalyptus	euphoric	neutrality	pneumonia	sleuth

Read the words aloud. Listen for the /ü/ or /yü/ sound.

Read these sentences. Notice the sound that the letter team *eu* has in the underlined words.

1. I tried to remain <u>neutral</u> as I listened to the men <u>feud</u>.
2. <u>Eugene</u> gave the <u>eulogy</u> at the funeral.
3. <u>Rheumatism</u> makes it hard for me to <u>maneuver</u> my fingers.
4. People were <u>euphoric</u> when the war ended.
5. <u>Pneumonia</u> is a disease of the lungs.

(Extra Practice, p. 184)

---EXCEPTIONS---

Europe (yŭr′əp)   museum (myü zē′əm)

Letter Team *ia*

/ē'ə/ media /ī'ə/ dial

The *ia* letter team will probably form parts of two separate syllables. In most words, the *i* will have the long *e* sound, and the *a* will have the schwa sound, as heard in *media*. In some words, the *i* will have a long *i* sound, and the *a* will have the schwa sound, as heard in *dial*.

Best Guess
for *ia* = long *e* followed by schwa
Second best guess = long *i* followed by schwa

Find four words that contain the letter team *ia*. Say the words. Notice the long *e* or the long *i* sound, followed by the schwa sound, in each.

diagnosis   mailbox   India   dialogue   dairy   Austria

Look at the words below. Each word contains the letter team *ia*. Read the words. Try the Best Guess. If you don't recognize a word, try the second best guess.

Arabian	cafeteria	diagram	hernia	memorial
bacteria	criteria	editorial	historian	trial
bias	denial	giant	liability	viable

Read the words aloud. Listen for the sound of the long *e* followed by schwa, or the long *i* followed by schwa.

Read these sentences. Notice the sound that letter team *ia* has in the underlined words.

1. Sylvia drew a diagram on the blackboard.

2. The custodian helped the librarian move the heavy boxes.

3. I read an editorial in an Austrian newspaper.

4. Take this vial of medicine to cure the bacterial infection.

5. The historian has found the diary of Paul Revere.

(Extra Practice, p. 184)

EXCEPTIONS

abbreviate (ə brē'vē āt)
The word *via* may be pronounced (vī'ə) or (vē'ə).

Letter Team *ie*

/ē/ **thief** /ī/ **pie** /ī'ə/ **diet**

The *ie* letter team will probably have the long *e* sound heard in *thief*. In some words, however, the *ie* letter team has the long *i* sound heard in *pie*. In a few words, the *ie* letter team forms parts of two separate syllables. In such words, the *i* will have a long *i* sound, and the *e* will have the schwa sound, as heard in *diet*.

Best Guess
for *ie* = long *e* /ē/
Second best guess = long *i* /ī/
Third best guess = long *i* followed by schwa

Find four words in which the letter team *ie* stands for the long *e* sound. Say the words.

brief   tied   their   relieve   Susie   niece

Find four words below in which the letter team *ie* stands for the long *i* sound. Say the words. What do the letters *ie* stand for in the other two words?

quiet   dried   ties   lies   client   dies

Now look at the words below. Each word contains the letter team *ie*. What vowel sound will *ie* probably stand for in each word? Try the Best Guess first. If you don't recognize some words, try the second and third best guesses. Read the words.

achieve	cookie	field	necktie	retrieve
belief	cried	untied	prairie	science
briefcase	diesel	grieve	priest	spies
chief	dieting	dries	quietly	yield

Read the words aloud. In each one, listen for the sound of long *e*, long *i*, or long *i* followed by schwa.

Now read the sentences on the next page.

Read these sentences. Notice the sound of long *e*, long *i*, or long *i* followed by schwa in the underlined words.

1. Debbie bought the supplies she needed to make brownies.

2. I cried with relief when I found my lost collie.

3. He has a variety of neckties.

4. I believe that fried foods should not be part of your diet.

5. The discovery of radium was a great achievement in science.

(Extra Practice, p. 185)

---EXCEPTIONS---

fiesta (fē es'tə)   sieve (siv)   view (vyü)
friend (frend)   Viet Nam (vē'et nam')
See Letter Team *ier*, p. 85.

Letter Teams *igh* and *ign*

/ī/ light /ī/ sign

When the vowel *i* is followed by *gh* or *gn*, it will probably have the long *i* sound heard in *light* and *sign*.

Best Guess
for *i* followed by *gh* or *gn* = long *i* /ī/

Find four words that have the letter team *igh* or *ign*. Say the words.

might   ghost   design   fright   benign   Ginny

Now look at the words below. Each word contains the letter team *igh* or *gn*. What sound will the vowel in each letter team probably have? Read the words.

align	delight	frighten	lightning	right
assign	designed	highlight	lighthouse	righteous
bright	fight	knight	mighty	sight
consignment	flight	light	resign	tighten

Read the words in the first two columns aloud. Listen for the sound of the long *i* in each word.

Read these sentences. Notice the long *i* sound in the underlined words.

. Bob played <u>tight</u> end on the <u>high</u> school football team.

. The front end of your car <u>might</u> be out of <u>alignment</u>.

. She painted the <u>highchair</u> a <u>bright</u> shade of yellow.

. I have a <u>slight</u> bruise on my <u>thigh</u>.

. He <u>resigned</u> as keeper of the <u>lighthouse</u>.

(Extra Practice, p. 185)

--- EXCEPTIONS ---

campaign (kam pān´)   See Letter Team *ei*, p. 59.

When *g* and *n* are in separate syllables, they are pronounced separately, and *i* is usually short:

signal (sig´ nəl)   significant (sig nif´ə kənt)   dignity (dig ni tē)

Letter Teams *oi* and *oy*

/oi/ boil, boy

When the vowel *o* is followed by *i* or *y*, it will probably have the /oi/ sound heard in *boil* and *boy*.

Best Guess
for *oi* and *oy* = /oi/ boil, boy

Find four words that have the letter team *oi* or *oy*. Say the words.

point   voyage   collie   oil   joy   Ollie

Now look at the words below. Each word contains the letter team *oi* or *oy*. What sound will each letter team probably have? Read the words.

annoy	coin	joyful	poison	toil
appoint	destroy	loyal	royal	toilet
avoid	employ	moist	soil	toy
broil	invoice	noise	spoil	void

Read the words aloud. Listen for the /oi/ sound in each one.

Now read these sentences. Notice the /oi/ sound in the underlined words.

1. <u>Joyce</u> spoke in a low <u>voice</u>.

2. <u>Roy</u> put <u>ointment</u> on the cut on his hand.

3. I hope that you will find your <u>choice</u> of hotels <u>enjoyable</u>.

4. <u>Moisten</u> your dry skin with <u>oil</u>.

5. He made an <u>appointment</u> to speak with his <u>employer</u>.

(Extra Practice, p. 186)

EXCEPTIONS

porpoise (pôr′pəs)   tortoise (tôr′təs)

Letter Team *oo*

/ü/ school /u̇/ book

The *oo* letter team often has the long *u* sound heard in *school*. In many words, however, the *oo* letter team has the /u̇/ sound heard in *book*.

Best Guess
for *oo* = long *u* /ü/
Second best guess = /u̇/ book

Find four words in which the letter team *oo* stands for the long *u* sound. Say the words.

noon   stop   stoop   coat   troop   broom

Find four words in which the letter team *oo* stands for the /u̇/ sound. Say the words.

look   good   god   wool   foot   won't

Now look at the words below. Each word contains the letter team *oo*. What vowel sound will *oo* probably stand for in each word? Try the Best Guess first. If you don't recognize a word, try the second best guess. Read the words.

afternoon	food	noose	room	stood
brook	goodbye	plywood	shampoo	took
cookies	groom	proof	shoot	tool
droop	moon	rookie	spool	zoom

Read the words aloud. Listen for the sounds that *oo* can have.

Read these sentences. Notice the sound *oo* has in each underlined word.

. The <u>whirlpool</u> made my tired back feel <u>good</u>.

. A <u>woodpecker</u> <u>stood</u> on the branch of the tree.

. Put a <u>teaspoon</u> of salt in the <u>mushroom</u> soup.

. I was <u>foolish</u> to try to ignore my <u>toothache</u>.

. <u>Smooth</u> the <u>wood</u> with sandpaper.

(Extra Practice, p. 186)

---EXCEPTIONS---

lood (blud)   brooch (brōch)   floor (flôr)

Letter Team *ou*

/ou/ out   /u/ young

The letter team *ou* usually has the /ou/ sound heard in *out*. In many words, however, *ou* has the short *u* sound heard in *young*.

Best Guess
for *ou* = /ou/   out
Second best guess = short *u* /u/

Find four words in which the *ou* letter team has the /ou/ sound. Say the words.

cloud	noon	noun	south	about	boot

Find four words in which the *ou* letter team has the /u/ sound. Say the words.

touch	tough	took	trouble	troop	rough

Now look at the words below. Each word contains the letter team *ou*. What sound will each letter team probably have? Try the Best Guess first. If you don't recognize a word, try the second best guess. Read the words.

around	couch	couple	house	sound
blouse	count	double	loud	thousand
bounce	country	doubt	roughen	touchdown
cloud	county	found	round	youngster

Read the words aloud. Listen for the /ou/ or /u/ sound in each word.

Now read these sentences. Notice the sound that *ou* has in each of the underlined words.

1. The <u>couple</u> rented a <u>house</u> in the <u>mountains</u>.

2. I'm <u>proud</u> to <u>announce</u> that the <u>trouble</u> is over.

3. My <u>cousin</u> wants to buy a <u>round</u>-trip ticket.

4. Will a <u>pound</u> of <u>flounder</u> be <u>enough</u> to serve two people?

5. The cat <u>pounced</u> on the <u>mouse</u>.

(Extra Practice, p. 187)

——EXCEPTIONS——

ought (bôt)   could (cu̇d)   group (grüp)
ough (kôf)   should (shu̇d)   soup (süp)
hought (thôt)   would (wu̇d)   through (thrü)

oulder (bōl′dər)   dough (dō)   though (thō)
houlder (shōl′dər)   soul (sōl)   thorough (thėr′ō)

he word *wound* may be pronounced (wünd) or (wound).

Letter Team *ow*

/ou/ cow   /ō/ snow

The letter team *ow* usually has the /ou/ sound heard in *cow*. In many words, however, *ow* has the long *o* sound heard in *snow*.

Best Guess
for *ow* = /ou/ cow
Second best guess = long *o* /ō/

Find four words in which *ow* has the /ou/ sound. Say the words.

wool   owl   how   spool   crown   vowel

Find four words in which *ow* has the long *o* sound. Say the words.

bowl   show   book   won   glow   throw

Now look at the words below. Each word contains the letter team *ow*. What sound will each letter team probably have? Try the Best Guess first. If you don't recognize a word, try the second best guess. Read the words.

allow	crowd	follow	mow	thrown
below	downtown	growl	powder	towed
clown	flow	growth	power	towel
crow	flower	however	slow	tower

Read the words aloud. Listen for the /ou/ or /ō/ sound in each word.

Now read these sentences. Notice the sound that *ow* has in each of the underlined words.

1. Buffalo Bill had a <u>renowned</u> <u>cowboy</u> <u>show</u>.

2. The <u>flowers</u> are <u>showing</u> a little new <u>growth</u>.

3. <u>How</u> strong is the <u>undertow</u> <u>down</u> at the beach today?

4. I want to take a <u>shower</u> before we go <u>bowling</u>.

5. She <u>owns</u> a <u>flowing</u> <u>brown</u> <u>gown</u>.

(Extra Practice, p. 187)

---EXCEPTIONS---

The word *bow* may be pronounced (bō) or (bou).
The word *sow* may be pronounced (sō) or (sou).

70

Vowel *o* with Other Consonants
/ô/ off

When the vowel *o* is followed by one or two consonants, it will usually have the short *o* sound heard in *hot*. However, in the letter team *off*, *oft*, *ong*, *oss*, *ost*, or *oth*, the vowel *o* may have a slightly different sound, as in the word *off*.

Best Guess
for *o* as in *off*, *oft*, *ong*, *oss*, *ost*, or *oth* = /ô/ off

---

Find the words that contain *off*, *oft*, *ong*, *oss*, *ost*, or *oth*. Say the words. Can you hear the /ô/ sound heard in *off*?

| song | hooting | frost | moth | toss | yolk | soft |

Now look at the words below. Look at the consonants that follow the *o* in each word. What vowel sound will you expect the vowel *o* to have? Read the words.

along	coffee	frosty	loss	offer
boss	cost	glossy	lost	often
broth	cross	loft	moss	softly
cloth	floss	long	moth	wrong

Read the words aloud. In each one, listen for the sound heard in *off*.

Read these sentences. Notice the sound the *o* has in each underlined word.

1. The police <u>officer</u> used to live <u>across</u> town.

2. <u>Moths</u> have chewed holes in my <u>tablecloth</u>.

3. <u>Ross</u> felt he had a <u>strong</u> chance of winning the race.

4. My <u>boss</u> <u>offered</u> me a better job.

5. <u>Often</u> it is hard to admit that you are <u>wrong</u>.

(Extra Practice, p. 188)

EXCEPTIONS

among (ə mung′)	gross (grōs)	most (mōst)
both (bōth)	host (hōst)	post (pōst)
clothes (klōz)	mammoth (mam′əth)	

See *l*-Controlled Vowels, pp. 72-73.

---

l-Controlled Vowels

/ô/ talk　/ī/ wild　/ō/ old

When the letter *l* follows the vowel *a* in a VCC pattern, the vowel sound will often be /ô/, as heard in *talk*. This happens especially when *a* is followed by *ll*, *lk*, and *lt*.

When the letters *ld* follow the vowel *i* in a VCC pattern, the vowel sound will usually be long *i*, as heard in *wild*.

When the letter *l* follows the vowel *o* in a VCC pattern, the vowel sound will probably be long *o*, as heard in *old*. This happens especially when *o* is followed by *ld*, *lk*, *lt*, and *ll*.

Best Guess
for *a* followed by *l* in VCC pattern = /ô/ talk
for *i* followed by *ld* in VCC pattern = long *i* /ī/
for *o* followed by *l* in VCC pattern = long *o* /ō/

Find four words in which the letter *l* follows *a*, *i*, or *o* in a VCC pattern. Say the words.

hall	lap	tale	told	colt	mild

Now look at the letters that make up the VCC pattern in the words below. In each word, the letter *l* controls the vowel sound.

all	chalk	gold	molt	stalk
alter	child	hall	old	stroll
although	colt	jolt	poll	told
bold	false	knoll	revolt	walk
bolt	fold	mold	salt	wild

Read the words aloud. Listen for the vowel sound in each word.

Now read the sentences. Notice how *l* affects the vowel sounds in the underlined words.

1. There were <u>golden</u> flowers on the <u>wallpaper</u>.

2. It was too <u>cold</u> for the <u>child</u> to go for a <u>walk</u>.

3. <u>All</u> of the <u>bolts</u> of <u>upholstery</u> fabric were on sale.

4. Jim <u>talks</u> <u>wildly</u> when he is excited.

5. <u>Always</u> use <u>potholders</u> or you will <u>scald</u> your hands.

(Extra Practice, p. 188)

Letter Team *ar*

/är/ car /er/ care /ar/ carry /ər/ dollar /ôr/ war

The letter team *ar* often has the /är/ sound heard in *car*. When the letter team *ar* is followed by the letter *e*, it will probably have the /er/ sound heard in *care*. When the letter team *ar* is followed by another *r*, it will probably have the /ar/ sound heard in *carry*.

Best Guess
for *ar* = /är/ car
for *ar* followed by *e* = /er/ care
for *ar* followed by *r* = /ar/ carry

Look at these words that have the letter team *ar*. What letter follows the *ar*? Say the words.

art   marry   star   stare   carrot   beware

Now look at the words below. Notice what letters follow the letter team *ar*. What sound will *ar* probably have? Read the words.

alarm	dare	harbor	market	sparrow
aware	farmer	Harry	parrot	stare
bare	flare	largest	rarely	wares
barrel	garden	mare	scare	yardstick

Read the words aloud. Listen for the different sounds the *ar* can have.

Read the sentences. Notice the sound *ar* has in each underlined word.

1. Barry will visit us in March.

2. Be careful when you carry the stoneware.

3. We found a jar of rare coins in the basement.

4. Who is your partner for the square dance?

5. The large sign said "Beware of the dog."

74

When *ar* appears in an unstressed syllable, the *a* will probably have the schwa sound heard in *dollar*. When *ar* follows either *w* or *qu*, it will probably have the /ôr/ sound heard in *war*.

Best Guess
for *ar* in an unstressed syllable = /ər/
for *ar* after *w* or *qu* = /ôr/ war

Find four words in which *ar* follows either *w* or *qu*. Say the words.

award   warm   altar   quart   quarter   cellar

Now look at the words below. Decide whether the *ar* appears in a stressed syllable. Look at what letter or letters the *ar* follows. What sound will the *ar* probably stand for in these words? Read the words.

calendar	separate	quarterly	ward	warp
collar	quarry	quartet	warmth	warranty
popular	quarter	quartz	warn	wart

Read the words aloud. Listen for the different sounds that *ar* stands for in these words.

Read these sentences. Notice the sound *ar* has in each underlined word.

1. Add a <u>quarter</u> cup of <u>sugar</u> to the batter.

2. During the <u>warm</u> weather, we make <u>regular</u> trips to the beach.

3. The instructor reviewed the <u>standard</u> rules of <u>grammar</u>.

4. The <u>quarry</u> is a <u>popular</u> place to swim.

5. The <u>quarterback</u> won an <u>award</u> as an outstanding player.

(Extra Practice, p. 189)

Letter Team *er*

/ėr/ term   /er/ very   /ər/ after   /ir/ here

The letter team *er* often has the /ėr/ sound heard in *term*. If the letter team *er* is followed by another *r* or by a vowel, though, it often has the /er/ sound heard in *very*. When *er* appears in an unstressed syllable, it will probably have the /ər/ sound heard in *after*. This sound is not very different from the /ėr/ sound heard in *term*.

Best Guess
for *er* = /ėr/ term
Second best guess = /er/ very

Best Guess
for *er* in an unstressed syllable = /ər/ after

Look at these words that have *er*. Say the words. Notice whether the *er* is in an unstressed syllable.

her	merit	farmer	corner	person	mercy

Now look at the words below. Look at the *er* in each word. Read the words. Try the Best Guesses first. If you don't recognize a word, try the second best guess.

alert	clerk	finger	kernel	serpent
anger	camper	germ	merchant	stereo
barber	clover	herd	mother	thunder
berry	danger	hunger	peril	terror
certain	Eric	Jerry	perish	tiger

Read the words aloud. Listen for the sound *er* has in each word.

Read these sentences. Notice the sound *er* has in each underlined word.

1. <u>Sterile</u> bandages will prevent the growth of <u>germs</u>.

2. We found the <u>perfect</u> spot for our picnic <u>under</u> a huge tree.

3. <u>Timber</u> is a leading product of <u>northern</u> Maine.

4. <u>Terry</u> wrote a <u>wonderful</u> <u>verse</u> in <u>her</u> writing class.

5. My <u>mother</u> and <u>father</u> own a house in New <u>Jersey</u>.

When the letter team *er* is part of either the VCV or the VVC long vowel pattern, it will probably have the /ir/ sound heard in *here* and *cheer*. The sound the *e* has is very similar to the long *e* sound.

Best Guess
for *er* in the VCV or VVC pattern = /ir/ here, cheer

Find four words in which *er* stands for the /ir/ sound. Say the words.

hero   queer   germ   red   mere   steer

Now look at the words below. Look at the letter that comes before or after the *er* in each word. What vowel sound will you expect the letter team *er* to have? Read the words.

austere	hereby	merely	pioneer	sheer
beer	jeer	peer	serious	sincere
cheerful	mere	period	severe	sphere

Read the words aloud. Listen for the sound that *er* has in each word.

Read these sentences. Notice the sound *er* has in each underlined word.

1. Hunters must <u>adhere</u> to the laws that control <u>deer</u> season.

2. <u>We're</u> going to <u>sincerely</u> miss you.

3. I would be <u>severely</u> sorry to get a <u>zero</u> on a test.

4. The <u>pioneers</u> crossed Lake <u>Superior</u> by raft.

5. Use <u>interior</u> paint inside the home, and <u>exterior</u> paint outside the home.

(Extra Practice, p. 189)

── EXCEPTIONS ──

heroine (her'ō ən)   were (wėr)
there (ҭHer)   where (hwer)

Letter Team *ir*

/ėr/ bird   /īr/ fire

The letter team *ir* usually has the /er/ sound heard in *bird*. However, when *ir* is followed by a vowel, as in the word *fire*, the vowel *i* has the long *i* sound.

Best Guess
for *ir* = /ėr/ bird
for *ir* followed by a vowel = /īr/ fire

Find two words in which *ir* stands for the /ėr/ sound heard in *bird*, and two words in which *ir* stands for the /īr/ sound heard in *fire*. Say the words.

sir   hired   thirty   hair   wire   ripple

Now look at the words below. Look at the letter that follows the *ir* in each word. What vowel sound will you expect the letter team *ir* to have? Read the words.

birch	dirt	pirate	stir	twirl
birthday	first	shirt	third	virus
circus	irate	siren	tirade	whirl
desire	iron	spiral	tire	wiring

Read the words aloud. Listen for the different vowel sounds heard in *bird* and *fire*.

Read these sentences. Notice the sound *ir* has in each underlined word.

1. A <u>firm</u> grip is <u>desirable</u> when you shake someone's hand.

2. Let me help you clean the <u>dirty</u> <u>fireplace</u>.

3. I went to the <u>circus</u> on my <u>thirteenth</u> <u>birthday</u>.

4. Your household <u>wiring</u> may be safer if you have a <u>circuit</u> breaker.

5. I need to <u>hire</u> a boy or <u>girl</u> to babysit for my son <u>Kirk</u>.

(Extra Practice, p. 190)

EXCEPTIONS

See Word Beginnings *il-*, *im-*, *in-*, *ir-*, p. 111.

Letter Team *or*

/ô/ for   /or/ sorry   /ər/ favor   /ėr/ word

The letter team *or* most often has the /ôr/ sound heard in *for*. However, if the letter team *or* is followed by another *r*, many people say the /or/ sound heard in *sorry*.

Best Guess
for *or* = /ôr/ for
for *or* followed by *r* = /or/ sorry

Find four words with the letter team *or*. Say the words.

before   horrible   port   road   borrow   barrel

Now look at the words below. What letter follows the *or*? What vowel sound will the letter team *or* have in each word? Read the words.

border	forward	morning	organ	sorrow
chord	horrid	normal	porridge	storage
corn	horse	north	score	tomorrow

Read the words aloud. Listen for the sounds heard in *for* and *sorry*.

Read these sentences. Notice the sound *or* has in each underlined word.

1. <u>Norman</u> needs to <u>borrow</u> a pair of <u>shorts</u>.

2. <u>Before</u> I leave <u>tomorrow</u>, I will <u>organize</u> my <u>correspondence</u> files.

3. I'm <u>sorry</u> that you found your trip to New <u>York</u> <u>boring</u>.

4. What is the <u>normal</u> <u>order</u> of events in your business day?

5. <u>Oregon</u> is in the <u>northwest</u> <u>corner</u> of the United States.

When the letter team *or* appears in an unstressed syllable, *or* will probably have the /ər/ sound heard in *favor*. When the letter team *or* follows the letter *w*, it will probably have the /ėr/ sound heard in *word*. These sounds are very similar.

Look at the Best Guess information on the next page.

Best Guess
for *or* in an unstressed syllable = /ər/ favor
for *or* after the letter *w* = /ėr/ word

Find three words in which the letter team *or* stands for the /ər/ sound. Say the words.

forge   actor   floor   color   odor

Find four words in which the letter team *or* stands for the /ėr/ sound. Say the words.

worm   roam   worst   raw   worth   work

Now look at the words below. What sound will the letter team *or* probably have? Read the words.

anchor	factor	humor	password	worse
armor	harbor	labor	trustworthy	worship
author	homework	manor	world	worthy

Read the words aloud. Listen for the different *or* sounds.

Read these sentences. Notice the sound *or* has in each underlined word.

1. Being an <u>actor</u> is hard <u>work</u>.

2. <u>Authors</u> must use their <u>words</u> carefully.

3. A person with <u>honor</u> is <u>trustworthy</u>.

4. Skunks give off the <u>worst</u> <u>odor</u>.

5. New York City is a <u>major</u> <u>harbor</u>.

(Extra Practice, p. 190)

Letter Team *ur*

/ėr/ fur   /ůr/ jury   /yůr/ pure   /ər/ picture

The letter team *ur* usually has the /er/ sound heard in *fur*. Sometimes, when a vowel comes after the letter team *ur*, the sound is the /ůr/ or /yůr/ sound heard in *jury* and *pure*.

Best Guess

for *ur* = /ėr/ fur

for *ur* followed by a vowel = /ůr/ or /yůr/ jury, pure

Find two words in which *ur* stands for the /ėr/ sound and two words in which *ur* stands for the /yůr/ sound. Say the words.

hurt   hunger   cure   furry   fury   hour

Now look at the words below. What letter follows the *ur*? What sound will you expect *ur* to have? Read the words.

burden	current	further	occur	rural
burst	durable	hurl	purify	surface
curfew	furnish	mural	purple	turkey
curing	furious	nurse	purpose	turn

Read the words aloud. Listen for the sound that *ur* has in each word.

Read these sentences. Notice the sound *ur* has in each underlined word.

. I <u>returned</u> to the <u>curb</u> when the traffic light changed.

. The woman wore a <u>turquoise</u> <u>turban</u>.

. On <u>Thursday</u>, I <u>splurged</u> and bought a new <u>purse</u>.

. The room was <u>furnished</u> with a bed and a <u>bureau</u>.

. The <u>curious</u> police officer <u>pursued</u> the <u>juror</u>.

When the letter team *ur* appears in an unstressed syllable, it will probably have the /ər/ sound heard in *picture*. This happens most often in words that end in *-ture*. In these words, the *t* has a /ch/ sound.

Look at the Best Guess information on the next page.

Best Guess
for *ur* in an unstressed syllable = /ər/

Find two words in which *ur* stands for the /ər/ sound. Say the words.

fixture   future   furnace   furl

Now look at the words below. In each one, the letter team *ur* appears in an unstressed syllable. Read the words.

adventure	denture	injure	nature	seizure
capture	feature	legislature	rupture	suture
creature	fracture	mixture	saturate	yogurt

Read the words aloud. Listen for the sound that *ur* has in each word.

Read these sentences. Notice the sound *ur* has in each underlined word.

1. Frankfurters often contain a mixture of different meats.

2. He gave a lecture on the beauty of nature.

3. This field is a natural pasture for cows.

4. Don't get injured by hot wires when you repair the fixture.

5. Paul Newman is featured in the picture now showing at the theater.

(Extra Practice, p. 191)

82

Letter Team *ear*

/ir/ ear   /ėr/ learn   /er/ bear

The letter team *ear* usually has the /ir/ sound heard in *ear*. However, in some words, *ear* has the /ėr/ sound heard in *learn*, and in a few words it has the /er/ sound heard in *bear*.

Best Guess
for *ear* = /ir/ ear
Second best guess = /ėr/ learn
Third best guess = /er/ bear

Look at the letter team *ear* in each word. Say the words. Notice the different sounds *ear* can stand for in these words.

dear   early   wear   hear   heard

Now look at the words below. What sound will you expect *ear* to have? Try the Best Guess first. If you don't recognize some words, try the second and third best guesses. Read the words.

appear	earn	learning	pearl	search
bearing	earth	near	rear	swear
clear	fear	pear	rehearse	year

Read the words aloud. Listen for the sound that *ear* has in each word.

Read these sentences. Notice the sound *ear* has in each underlined word.

1. Are you fearful of earthquakes?

2. Wear something nice for your yearbook picture.

3. I heard that they are tearing down that old building.

4. The play rehearsal is nearly over.

5. He swears that he is fearless.

(Extra Practice, p. 191)

--- EXCEPTIONS ---

heart (hart)
The word *tear* may be pronounced (tir) or (ter).

Letter Teams *air* and *eir*

/er/ hair /er/ their

The letter team *air* usually has the /er/ sound heard in *hair*. The letter team *eir* often has the same /er/ sound, as in *their*.

Best Guess
for *air* or *eir* = /er/ hair, their

Find three words in which *air* stands for the /er/ sound and one word in which *eir* stands for the /er/ sound. Say the words.

heir   affair   friar   fair   pair   rail

Now look at the words below. What sound will you expect *air* or *eir* to have? Read the words.

airplane	debonair	fairly	heiress	repair
chair	despair	fairy	impair	stair
dairy	eclair	flair	paired	theirs

Read the words aloud. Listen for the sound of *air* or *eir*.

Read these sentences. Note the sound *air* or *eir* has in each underlined word.

1. From the airplane, I had a wonderful view of the prairie.

2. Claire is dusting their staircase.

3. The dairy was selling milk and butter at the fair.

4. I have a pair of fairly new books.

5. Move your chair closer to the air conditioner.

(Extra Practice, p. 192)

Letter Team *ier*

/ē′ər/ happier   /ī′ər/ flier   /ir/ pier

The letter team *ier* generally forms parts of different syllables and usually has the /ē′ər/ sound heard in *happier*. In some words, the *ier* letter team has the long *i* sound followed by /ər/, as in *flier*. In a few words, *ier* has the /ir/ sound heard in *pier*.

Best Guess
for *ier* = /ē′ər/ happier
Second best guess = /ī′ər/ flier
Third best guess = /ir/ pier

Look at the words. Find one word in which *ier* has the /ir/ sound heard in *pier*. Notice in the other words that *ier* forms parts of two syllables. Say all the words.

drier   fierce   funnier   grumpier   rainier   pliers

Now look at the words below. What sound will you expect *ier* to have? Try the Best Guess first. If you don't recognize some words, try the second and third best guesses. Read the words.

bumpier	dirtier	fierce	needier	prettier
cashier	easier	frier	piercing	rainier
crier	emptier	friendlier	pliers	supplier

Read the words aloud. Listen for the sound that *ier* has in each word.

Read these sentences. Notice the sound *ier* has in each underlined word.

1. Please order some more <u>copier</u> paper from the <u>supplier</u>.

2. The lion was always <u>fierce</u>, but today he seemed <u>angrier</u> than usual.

3. It was <u>windier</u> out on the <u>pier</u> than it was on the shore.

4. The <u>flier</u> was assigned duty on an aircraft <u>carrier</u>.

5. She quit her job as a diner <u>cashier</u> to work in a <u>fancier</u> restaurant.

(Extra Practice, p. 192)

— EXCEPTION —

soldier (sōl′jər)

Mixed Review

Practice what you have learned by reading these sentences.

1. Claire took an airplane to Hong Kong.
2. The losses that the fire caused were costly.
3. My boss told me that I would have a secure future as a cashier.
4. John Foss is the author of some fairly good war stories.
5. At an earlier game last season, the Bears lost by one point.
6. The priest took food to the hurricane victims.
7. Susie met Larry during her flight to Austria.
8. From across the prairie, we saw signs of a lightning storm.
9. Perry tossed the car keys into a bowl on top of the refrigerator.
10. He has a purple bruise where he injured his ear.
11. I think that her hair was prettier before she had it frosted.
12. We will be in Australia from Thursday to Sunday.
13. I can't repair the lawn mower until I search for my missing pliers.
14. My daughter Terry is away at a play rehearsal this afternoon.
15. The boss has an appointment to interview thirty fliers today.
16. The child yawned as he crawled up the stairs to bed.
17. I'm very sorry that they moved away to northern Maine.
18. The audience cheered as the curtain came down to end the show.
19. I have never seen a dirtier fireplace.
20. Put a pat of butter on your bowl of porridge to make it taste better.
21. The circuit blew because the wires were crossed.
22. The land will erode if the yew trees decay and fall down.
23. To my despair, I learned that Ross died on Tuesday.
24. I often hear the songs of birds outside my window in the morning.
25. We will serve dinner to the crew after the rehearsal.

The letters *c* and *g* are consonants. A consonant usually stands for one sound. *C* and *g* are special, though, because each letter can stand for several sounds. We say that *c* or *g* has a **hard** sound or a **soft** sound at times. At other times *c* or *g* may team up with other letters to make whole new sounds. *C* and *g* may even sound like other letters. This part of the handbook will teach you the sounds that *c* and *g* can have.

How many of these sounds do you already know? Read the list below. The key words will help you know the sounds that *c* and *g* can stand for.

cape	/k/	page 89	**ch**ef	/sh/	page 93
cell	/s/	page 90	**g**ame	/g/	page 95
oc**c**ur	/k/	page 91	a**g**e	/j/	page 96
su**cc**ess	/ks/	page 91	**gh**ost	/g/	page 98
dis**c**	/sk/	page 92	ni**ght**	/silent gh/	page 98
s**c**ene	/s/	page 92	lau**gh**	/f/	page 98
chip	/ch/	page 93	**gu**ess	/g/	page 99
chord	/k/	page 93	lan**gu**age	/gw/	page 99

Hard c

/k/ cape

The letter *c* usually stands for the /k/ sound you hear at the beginning of the word *cape*. This sound is called the hard sound of *c*. Unless *c* is followed by *e*, *i*, or *y*, it usually stands for the hard sound.

Best Guess
for *c* = hard *c* /k/

Find four words in which *c* is followed by any letter other than *e*, *i*, or *y*, or by no letter. Say the words.

crank   certain   create   picnic   trick   traced

Look at the list of words below. Look at each *c*. What letter, if any, follows it? What sound do you expect *c* to stand for? Now read the words.

acrid	copper	cute	fleck	panic
acute	crest	decade	lucky	uncle
attic	crying	fact	narcotic	vacate
clip	curious	factory	nickel	victim

Read the first two columns of words aloud. Listen for the hard sound of *c*. Notice where you hear it in each word.

Now read these sentences. Notice the letters that come after *c*.

1. I like the <u>copper</u>-<u>colored</u> <u>curtains</u> best.

2. We must <u>conserve</u> and take <u>care</u> of the earth.

3. The <u>electrical</u> storm <u>caused</u> the fire.

4. The <u>cooking</u> oil is in the <u>can</u> next to the <u>cream</u>.

5. A <u>decade</u> ago, this <u>couple</u> got married.

(Extra Practice, p. 193)

Soft *c*

/s/ cell

When the letter *c* is followed by an *e, i,* or *y,* it usually stands for the /s/ sound you hear at the beginning of *cell.* This sound is called the soft sound of *c.*

Best Guess
for *c* followed by *e, i,* or *y* = soft c /s/

Find four words in which *c* is followed by *e, i,* or *y.* Say the words.

celery   call   traced   vocal   spicy   dancing

Look at the list of words below. Look at each letter *c.* What letter follows it? What sound do you expect *c* to stand for? Now read the words.

acid	citizen	fancy	necessary	process
brace	decent	icing	nice	recipe
ceiling	decide	icy	police	sentence
cider	exercise	mercy	precise	tricycle

Read the last two columns of words aloud. Listen for the soft sound of *c.* Notice where you hear it in each word.

Now read these sentences. Notice the letters that come after *c.*

1. I was <u>excited</u> to find the <u>bracelet</u> I lost!

2. What is the <u>distance</u> between those <u>cities</u>?

3. We found it <u>necessary</u> to build a new <u>facility</u>.

4. <u>Citrus</u> fruits are so <u>nice</u> and <u>juicy</u>!

5. Are you <u>certain</u> that the <u>ceremony</u> starts at noon?

(Extra Practice, p. 193)

— EXCEPTIONS —

ocean (ō'shən)   special (spesh'əl)

Consonants *cc*

/k/ occur   /ks/ success

When the letters *cc* are followed by any letter except *e, i,* or *y,* they usually stand for the /k/ sound you hear in *occur.* When the letters *cc* are followed by *e, i,* or *y,* they usually have the /ks/ sound heard in *success.*

Best Guess
for *cc* = hard *c* /k/
for *cc* followed by *e, i,* or *y* = /ks/

Find two words in which the letters *cc* are followed by *e, i,* or *y.* Say the words.

| accord | vaccine | accuse | raccoon | accent | hiccup |

Look at the list of words below. Look at each *cc.* What letter follows these letters? What sound do you expect *cc* to stand for? Now read the words.

accompany	accumulate	accustomed	occasion	occupy
account	accurate	broccoli	occupant	tobacco
accountant	accuse	moccasin	occupation	zucchini

What letter follows the *cc* in each of these words?

| accelerate | accept | succeed | accident | vaccinate |

Read all the words aloud. Listen for the two sounds that *cc* can have. Notice where you hear them in the words.

Now read these sentences. Notice the letters that come after *cc.*

1. A raccoon ate the broccoli in our garden.

2. The other party accepted our accident report.

3. Do not accelerate when the light turns yellow.

4. The doctor hoped the vaccine would succeed in keeping us healthy.

5. I am not accustomed to having such succulent steak.

(Extra Practice, p. 194)

--- EXCEPTION ---

soccer (sok′ər)

Consonants _sc_

/sk/ disc   /s/ scene

When the letters _sc_ are followed by any letter except _e, i,_ or _y,_ they usually stand for the /sk/ sound you hear in _disc._ When the letters _sc_ are followed by _e, i,_ or _y,_ they usually have the /s/ sound you hear in the word _scene._

Best Guess
for _sc_ = /sk/
for _sc_ followed by _e, i,_ or _y_ = soft _c_ /s/

Find two words in which _sc_ is followed by _e, i,_ or _y._ Say the words.

scab   science   descend   scrap   school   scuba

Look at the list of words below. Look at each _sc._ What letter follows these letters? What sound do you expect _sc_ to stand for? Now read the words.

discuss	scar	schedule	Scotland	screen
escape	scarf	scholar	scrape	scribble
scale	scatter	score	scratch	unscrew

In these words, what letters follow _sc?_ Say the words.

adolescent   fascinate   fluorescent   scent   scissors

Read all the words aloud. Listen for the two sounds of _sc._ Notice where you hear them in the words.

Now read these sentences. Notice the letters that come after _sc._

1. Peter escorted us when we met the sculptor.

2. You can buy this prescription at a discount drug store.

3. Describe the scenery that you liked best.

4. I discovered that the scissors had fallen under the table.

5. No one could read the notes that the scholar had scribbled.

(Extra Practice, p. 194)

EXCEPTIONS

conscience (kon'shəns)   muscle (mus'əl)   schwa (shwä)

Consonants *ch*

/ch/ chip   /k/ chord   /sh/ chef

The letters *ch* usually have the /ch/ sound that you hear in *chip*. The letters can also sound like /k/, as in *chord*, or like /sh/, as in *chef*.

Best Guess
for *ch* = /ch/
Second best guess = /k/
Third best guess = /sh/

Find the four words that contain the letters *ch*. Say the words.

scorn   chin   witch   echo   clean   chute

Look at the list of words below. In all these words, the Best Guess is the right guess. Now read the words.

chain	chant	chase	child	chipped
chair	chapped	cheap	children	chocolate
challenge	chapter	cheat	China	choose
chance	charge	checkbook	Chinese	churches
channel	charm	cheese	chipmunk	churn

Read the last two columns of words aloud. Listen for the /ch/ sound. In which word do you hear it twice?

Now read these sentences. Notice the *ch* in each of the underlined words.

1. Warm your <u>chapped</u> hands over the <u>charcoal</u> fire.

2. You have a <u>choice</u> of <u>cherry</u> or lime pie.

3. <u>Which</u> <u>chores</u> have you done?

4. You will <u>chuckle</u> when you hear how badly I speak <u>French</u>.

5. You can <u>charge</u> this <u>merchandise</u> if you wish.

Go on to the next page.

Look at the list of words below. In all these words, the second best guess for *ch* is the right guess. Now read the words.

ache	character	chorus	chronicle	monarch
anchor	chemist	chrome	echo	monarchy
chaos	chemistry	chronic	mechanic	stomach

Read the words aloud and listen for the /k/ sound. Notice where you hear the sound in each word.

Look at the words below. Many of them come from the French language. The third best guess for *ch* is the right guess for these. Try to read them.

| brochure | chaperon | chef | chute | machinery |
| chagrin | charade | chevron | machine | Michigan |

Read each group of words aloud. In each group, listen for the /sh/ sound. Notice where you hear it in each word.

Now read these sentences. If you have trouble with a word, try a different sound for *ch*.

1. Is the <u>chef</u> named <u>Chris</u> or <u>Charlie</u>?

2. <u>Mocha</u> tastes like <u>chocolate</u> and coffee.

3. The <u>mechanic</u> fixed the wheel but not the <u>chrome</u> hubcap.

4. An awful <u>stench</u> filled the <u>chemistry</u> lab.

5. Have you ever played the game of <u>charades</u>?

(Extra Practice, p. 195)

EXCEPTIONS

Chanukah (ha'nə kə)   chutzpah (huts'pə)

Hard *g*

/g/ game

The letters *g* and *gg* usually stand for the /g/ sound you hear at the beginning of the word *game*. This sound is called the hard sound of *g*. If a single *g* is followed by any letter other than *e*, *i*, or *y*, the *g* is usually hard. Words ending with hard *g* keep the hard sound even when *er*, *ing*, or *y* are added to them. For example, you hear a hard *g* in *dig* and *digger*, even though *digger* has an *e* after the *g*.

> **Best Guess**
> for *g* = hard *g* /g/

Find four words in which *g* is followed by no letter, or by any letter besides *e*, *i*, or *y*. Say the words.

bag	igloo	cage	glass	goal	magic

Look at the list of words below. Look at each *g*. What letter, if any, follows it? What sound do you expect *g* to stand for? Now read the words.

druggist	fragment	glare	hugs	legal
eggnog	gash	glue	jog	organ
foggy	glasses	graze	jogger	wiggle

Read the last two columns of words aloud. Listen for the hard *g* sound. Notice where you hear it in each word.

Now read these sentences. Notice the letters that come after *g*.

1. A piece of <u>glass</u> covered the old <u>flag</u>.

2. The <u>biggest</u> <u>goalie</u> is the <u>youngest</u> player.

3. We can <u>organize</u> the <u>games</u> so everyone has a chance to play.

4. This was the <u>foggiest</u> day I've ever seen in <u>August</u>.

5. Eric <u>grabbed</u> the <u>magnet</u> from the shelf.

(Extra Practice, p. 195)

—— EXCEPTION ——

exaggerate (eg zaj′ə rāt′)

Soft g

/j/ age

When the letter *g* is followed by an *e, i,* or *y,* it usually has the /j/ sound you hear in *age.* This sound is called the soft *g* sound. When the letter team *ge* follows *d,* the *d* is silent. For example, you hear the soft *g* in *bridge* but not the *d.* Some words with *ge, gi,* and *gy* still keep the hard *g* sound. Try that sound next.

Best Guess
for *g* followed by *e, i,* or *y* = soft *g* /j/
Second best guess = hard *g* /g/

Find four words in which *g* is followed by *e, i,* or *y.* Say the words.

genius   ginger   urge   grab   guess   stingy

Look at the list of words below. Look at each letter *g.* What letter follows it? What sound do you expect *g* to stand for? In all these words, *g* has a soft sound. Now read the words.

badge	gelatin	gin	image	large
edge	gems	gymnasium	imagine	manage
forge	gerbil	gypsum	intelligent	origin
fudge	germ	hedge	judge	page

Read the middle three columns of words aloud. Listen for the soft sound of *g.* Notice where you hear it in each word.

Now read these sentences. Notice the letters that come after *g* in the underlined words.

1. The <u>surgeon</u> <u>urged</u> me to rest for a week.

2. Do not stand near the <u>edge</u> of that <u>ledge</u>!

3. The <u>ranger</u> saved us from a <u>tragic</u> fate.

4. Have you ever had <u>genuine</u> home-made <u>ginger</u> ale?

5. Someone with <u>knowledge</u> of that <u>region</u> can help you.

Now look at this list of words. Here, the second best guess for _ge, gi,_ or _gy_ is the right guess. Read the words.

anger	forget	Geiger	giggle	gizzard
begin	forgive	gelding	Gilbert	gynecology
eager	gear	get	gild	hunger
finger	geese	gift	give	together

Read all the words aloud and listen for the hard sound of _g._ Do you hear the sound at the beginning, middle, or end of the word?

Now read these sentences. If you have trouble with a word, try a different sound for _g._

. Eat one of those <u>large</u> apples if you are <u>hungry</u>.

. Let's all chip in and <u>give</u> one big <u>gift</u>.

. Don't <u>forget</u> that Sue is <u>allergic</u> to <u>garlic</u>.

. This book will <u>give</u> you a <u>good</u> <u>general</u> sense of the time.

. This bike has <u>gears</u>, so <u>getting</u> up hills is easy.

(Extra Practice, p. 196)

Consonants *gh*

/g/ ghost   /silent gh/ night   /f/ laugh

The letters *gh* usually have the hard *g* sound if they begin a word. They are often silent in the middle of a word or at the end. Sometimes, at the end of a word, they sound like /f/, as in *laugh*.

Best Guess
for *gh* at the beginning of a word = /g/
for *gh* in the middle of a word = /silent gh/
for *gh* at the end of a word = /silent gh/
Second best guess for *gh* at the end of a word = /f/

Look at the list of words below. Notice where the letters *gh* are in each word. What sound do you expect them to have? In all these words, the Best Guess for *gh* is the right guess. Now read the words.

bought	fought	ghoul	sigh	though
delight	fright	might	slight	thought
dough	ghetto	night	thigh	through

In these words, the second best guess is correct. Read the words.

cough	enough	laugh	rough	tough

Read all the words aloud. Listen for the sound of *gh*. In which words do you hear the letters? In which words are the letters silent?

Read these sentences. Notice where the letters *gh* are in each word.

1. You <u>ought</u> to see a doctor about that <u>cough</u>.

2. We <u>bought</u> the car when we had saved <u>enough</u> money.

3. Does that dog <u>weigh eighty</u> pounds?

4. We had a <u>ghastly flight</u> because of the storm.

5. No one has ever <u>caught</u> a <u>ghost</u>, except in movies.

(Extra Practice, p. 196)

--- EXCEPTION ---

spaghetti (spə get′ē)

gu + Vowels

/g/ guess   /gw/ language

When the letters *gu* are followed by a vowel, the *g* is usually a hard *g*. The *u* is silent, but the next vowel is not. For instance, you do not hear the *u* in *guess*, but you do hear the *e*. When the letters *gue* come at the end of a word, you hear only hard *g*. In some words, *gu* followed by a vowel may have the /gw/ sound you hear in *language*.

Best Guess
for *gu* followed by a vowel = hard *g* + the vowel
Second best guess = /gw/

Best Guess
for *gue* at the end of a word = hard *g* /g/

Find two words in which *gue* is at the end of a word. Say the words.

| guilt | guarantee | plague | guess | guest | vague |

Look at the list of words below. What letter follows each *gu*? Notice where you see the letters in each word. In all these words, the right guess is the Best Guess for *gu* followed by a vowel. Now read the words.

disguise	guard	guide	guitar	morgue
epilogue	guess	guild	intrigue	synagogue
guarantee	guest	guilt	monologue	vogue

Read the middle three columns of words aloud. Listen for the hard sound of *g*. Where do you hear it in each word?

Now read the words below. Here the second best guess for *gu* followed by a vowel is right.

| anguish | extinguish | Guatemala | iguana | languish |
| distinguish | Guam | jaguar | language | linguini |

Read the words aloud and listen for the /gw/ sound. Notice where you hear it in each word.

Now go on to the next page.

Read these sentences. If you have trouble with a word, try a different sound for *gu*.

1. My car is <u>guaranteed</u> against rust for one year.

2. She used sign <u>language</u> to instruct the deaf students.

3. The best player in the <u>league</u> was <u>guilty</u> of foul play.

4. The governor was our <u>distinguished</u> <u>guest</u>.

5. The show opened with a funny <u>monologue</u> by a new comic.

(Extra Practice, p. 197)

——— EXCEPTION ———

argue (är′gyü)

Mixed Review

Practice what you have learned by reading these sentences.

1. I wear glasses only when I read.
2. Pam's second guess was correct.
3. A gherkin is sweeter than a sour pickle.
4. We went to three cities in four days.
5. You will succeed if you try hard.
6. The report in the newspaper was accurate.
7. Many people come to jog on this track after work.
8. Don't burn your tongue on the pizza.
9. We have to cut the grass every week.
10. You can paint scenery if you do not want to act in the play.
11. My mother is a chemist for a big company.
12. The jaguar is a member of the cat family.
13. Turn left after you walk through the door.
14. General Adams spoke to the troops.
15. Put up screens so no bugs get in.
16. The camp sent us a brochure that showed the cabins.
17. All the children spoke at once.
18. This meat is too tough to chew.
19. May I have your recipe for chili?
20. A magnet will pick up all those pins.
21. The class will discuss the story when we finish reading it.
22. Everyone can sing the chorus together.
23. The last goal won the game.
24. A budget will help you save money.
25. This month my electric bill was very low.

Many long words are really just short words with beginnings and endings added to them. For example, the word *rereading* is just the word *read* with a beginning and ending added on. The letters *re-* are the beginning. The letters *-ing* are the ending.

re + read + ing

A word part that is added to the beginning of a word is called a **prefix**. Prefixes have meanings. When you add them to words, you change the meanings of those words. For example, the prefix *re-* means "again." The word *reread* means "read again."

To read a prefix, you must first recognize it. How can you tell if a word has a prefix? One way is to see whether the word makes sense without those letters. Take *re-* away from *retie* and you have the word *tie*. But take *re-* away from *rested* and you do not have a word that makes sense. At the same time many prefixes, such as *ad-* in *admit*, are not easy to recognize. They will become more familiar over time.

Recognizing word endings can also help you read long words. Many word endings are **suffixes**. Like prefixes, when you add suffixes to words, you change the words. Suffixes change how words are used. When you add *-ous* to *danger* and make *dangerous*, you change a word that names something into a word that can tell about or describe something.

Some word endings look hard to read, but many are really quite simple once you learn the patterns. For example, when you learn that *-tion*, *-cian*, and *-ssion* can all have the same sound, you can read many words easily. In the Appendix, you can learn the meanings of many suffixes and prefixes.

Read over this list of beginnings and endings, continued on the next page. See how many of these word parts you already know. The key words can help you.

admit	/ad/	page 105	**committee**	/kə/	page 108
adore	/əd/	page 105	**contribution**	/ko/	page 108
antidote	/an ti/	page 106	**de**sign	/di/	page 109
antiaircraft	/an tē/	page 106	**de**code	/dē/	page 109
become	/bi/	page 107	**ex**cellent	/eks/	page 109
biannual	/bī/	page 107	**ex**act	/egz/	page 109
cooperate	/kō/	page 108	**hyper**active	/hī pər/	page 109

illegal	/il/	page 111	ambulance	/əns/	page 125
imbalance	/im/	page 111	difference	/əns/	page 125
incomplete	/in/	page 111	important	/ənt/	page 126
irregular	/ir/	page 111	excellent	/ənt/	page 126
megaphone	/meg ə/	page 112	locate	/āt/	page 127
microwave	/mī krō/	page 112	pirate	/it/	page 127
microscope	/mī krə/	page 112	hunted	/ed/	page 128
minibike	/min ē/	page 112	begged	/d/	page 128
minimal	/min ə/	page 112	walked	/t/	page 128
nonfiction	/non/	page 114	machine	/ēn/	page 129
permission	/pər/	page 114	imagine	/ən/	page 129
permanent	/pėr/	page 114	communism	/iz əm/	page 130
polygon	/pol ē/	page 115	sarcasm	/az əm/	page 130
postpone	/pōst/	page 115	unity	/ə tē/	page 131
prepare	/pri/	page 116	society	/ə tē/	page 131
prearrange	/prē/	page 116	active	/iv/	page 132
prejudice	/pre/	page 116	arrive	/īv/	page 132
promote	/prə/	page 116	circle	/əl/	page 133
program	/prō/	page 116	little	/l/	page 133
promise	/pro/	page 116	famous	/əs/	page 134
reappear	/rē/	page 118	pleasure	/zhər/	page 135
recover	/ri/	page 118	pressure	/shər/	page 135
recommend	/re/	page 118	usual	/zhü əl/	page 135
subway	/sub/	page 119	sensual	/shü əl/	page 135
submerge	/səb/	page 119	nation	/shən/	page 136
superman	/sü pər/	page 119	passion	/shən/	page 136
synonym	/sin/	page 119	vision	/zhən/	page 137
uncooked	/un/	page 121	tension	/shən/	page 137
unicycle	/yü nə/	page 121	partial	/shəl/	page 138
telephone	/tel ə/	page 121	patient	/shənt/	page 138
adorable	/ə bəl/	page 122	electrician	/shən/	page 138
possible	/ə bəl/	page 122	appreciate	/shē āt/	page 138
privacy	/ə sē/	page 123	conscience	/shəns/	page 138
fantasy	/ə sē/	page 123	conscious	/shəs/	page 138
garbage	/ij/	page 124	nature	/chər/	page 141
garage	/äzh/	page 124	actual	/chü əl/	page 141

Word Beginning *ad-*

/ad/ admit /ə d/ adore

The prefix *ad-* usually has the /ad/ sound and stands for one syllable at the beginning of a word. Can you hear the /ad/ sound at the beginning of the word *admit*? In some words that begin with *ad-*, the letter *a* stands for the schwa sound and is said as a syllable by itself. The letter *d* starts the second syllable with the /d/ sound. Can you hear the /ə/ sound in the first syllable of the word *adore*?

Best Guess
for *ad-* at the beginning of a word = /ad/
Second best guess = /ə d/

Look at each word and its beginning. What sound do you expect the prefix *ad-* to stand for at the beginning of each word? In all these words, the Best Guess is the right guess. Read the words.

addict	admire	adolescent	adversary	advice
adequate	admission	advantage	adverse	advise
adhesive	admonish	adventure	advertise	advocate

In the words below, the second best guess is correct.

adapt	adept	adopt	adorable	adrift
addition	ado	adoption	adorn	adult

Read all the words aloud. Listen for the sound of the prefix *ad-*.

Now read these sentences. If you have trouble with a word, try a different sound for the *ad-* beginning.

1. It will be to your <u>advantage</u> to <u>adhere</u> to all the rules.

2. <u>Adults</u> like to give <u>adolescents</u> <u>advice</u>.

3. The agency will <u>administer</u> the baby's <u>adoption</u>.

4. I <u>admire</u> someone who is so <u>adept</u> at writing <u>advertising</u> slogans.

(Extra Practice, p. 197)

--- EXCEPTIONS ---

adjective (aj′ik tiv)   adjust (ə just′)
The word *address* may be pronounced (ə dres′) or (ad′res).

105

Word Beginnings *anti-* and *ante-*

/an ti/ antidote   /an tē/ antiaircraft

When the prefixes *anti-* and *ante-* come before a consonant, they usually have the /an ti/ sound heard in the word *antidote*. When *anti-* comes before a vowel, it stands for the /an tē/ sound. In the word *antiaircraft*, you can hear the /an tē/ sound at the beginning of the word. Sometimes, for emphasis, *anti-* can have the /an tī/ sound.

Best Guess
for *anti-* and *ante-* followed by a consonant = /an ti/
for *anti-* followed by a vowel = /an tē/

Find two words in which *anti-* is followed by a vowel. Say all the words.

anticipate	antiunion	antiaircraft	antihero

Look at each word below. Look at each beginning. What sound do you expect *anti-* or *ante-* to stand for at the beginning of each word? Now read the words.

antebellum	antibiotic	anticlimax	antihistamine	antipathy
antechamber	antibody	antidepressant	antiknock	antisocial
anteroom	anticipation	antidote	antimagnetic	antithesis
antibacterial	anticlimactic	antifreeze	antipasto	antitoxin

Read all the words aloud. Listen for the sound of *anti-* or *ante-*. Also, notice how the stress is different in *antipathy* and *antithesis* from the other words.

Now read these sentences. Notice whether a vowel or a consonant comes after the prefix in each underlined word.

1. He waited in the <u>anteroom</u> outside the King's private bedroom.

2. The doctor prescribed an <u>antidepressant</u> drug.

3. In <u>anticipation</u> of the holidays, we decorated the house.

4. The <u>antebellum</u> homes are the <u>antithesis</u> of log cabins.

5. We ordered <u>antipasto</u> to begin our meal.

(Extra Practice, p. 198)

——EXCEPTIONS——

antecedent (an'tə sēd'nt)   antiseptic (an'tə sep'tik)

Word Beginnings *be-* and *bi-*

/bi/ become   /bī/ biannual

The word beginning *be-* usually has the /bi/ sound, and it stands for one syllable at the beginning of a word. Can you hear the /bi/ sound at the beginning of the word *become*? The prefix *bi-* usually has the /bī/ sound, and it stands for one syllable. You can hear the /bī/ sound in the word *biannual*.

Best Guess
for *be-* at the beginning of a word = /bi/
for *bi-* at the beginning of a word = /bī/

Look at each word below. Look at the beginning of each word. What sound do you expect *be-* to stand for in each word? Read the words.

because	before	behalf	below	betake
become	befriend	behind	bemoan	beware
befall	begin	belabor	bestow	bewitch

Now read these words. What sound do you expect *bi-* to stand for?

| bicentennial | bicuspid | bilateral | biopsy | bivalve |
| biceps | bicycle | bimonthly | bipartisan | biweekly |

Read all the words aloud. Listen for the sound that *be-* and *bi-* stand for at the beginning of each word.

Now read these sentences. Notice the letters that begin each underlined word.

1. As the storm approached, the wind <u>began</u> to howl.

2. <u>Beware</u> that you do not put your finger too near a <u>bivalve</u>.

3. They print a <u>bimonthly</u> newsletter about local events.

4. On <u>behalf</u> of all your friends, I present you with this <u>bicycle</u>.

5. He <u>bemoans</u> the fact that he has small <u>biceps</u>.

(Extra Practice, p. 198)

Word Beginning *co-*

/kō/ cooperate   /kə/ committee   /ko/ contribution

The prefix *co-* usually has the /kō/ sound heard in *cooperate*. When *co-* comes before the consonant *l*, *m*, or *n*, it usually stands for the /kə/ sound heard in *committee*. Sometimes *co-* stands for the /ko/ sound heard in *contribution*.

Best Guess
for *co-* at the beginning of a word = /kō/
for *co-* followed by *l*, *m*, or *n* at the beginning of a word = /kə/
Second best guess for *co-* = /ko/

Look at the beginning of each word below. What letter follows *co-*? What sound do you expect the prefix to stand for in each word? The Best Guess for each word is correct. Now read the words.

coauthor	collaboration	combine	concern	coordinate
coconut	collateral	community	condemn	copayment
codefendant	collection	companion	condition	cosponsor
coincide	collide	conceal	conservative	covert

In the words below, the second best guess is correct.

| colony | compliment | compromise | confidential | continent |
| combination | composition | concrete | consequence | cosmetic |

Read all the words aloud. Listen for the sound that *co-* stands for in each word.

Now read these sentences. If you have trouble with a word, try saying the prefix with a different sound.

1. It's a <u>coincidence</u> that we both joined the <u>conservation</u> <u>committee</u>.

2. Have you <u>considered</u> electing <u>cocaptains</u> for the volleyball team?

3. The <u>conspirators</u> decided to <u>cooperate</u> with the authorities.

4. The writer <u>continues</u> to <u>collect</u> <u>colloquial</u> sayings for her book.

5. The <u>cosmetic</u> <u>company</u> is a <u>cosponsor</u> of the road race.

(Extra Practice, p. 199)

---EXCEPTIONS---

comfort (kum'fərt)   correspond (kôr'ə spond')

Word Beginnings *de-*, *ex-*, and *hyper-*

/di/ design   /dē/ decode   /eks/ excellent   /egz/ exact
/hī pər/ hyperactive

The prefix *de-* usually stands for the /di/ sound heard at the beginning of *design*. Sometimes, *de-* stands for the /dē/ sound heard at the beginning of *decode*. The prefix *ex-* usually has the /eks/ sound heard in *excellent*. When *ex-* is followed by a vowel, it sometimes stands for the /egz/ sound heard in *exact*. The prefix *hyper-* is said /hī pər/, as in *hyperactive*.

Best Guess
for *de-* at the beginning of a word = /di/
Second best guess = /dē/

Best Guess
for *ex-* at the beginning of a word = /eks/
Second best guess = /egz/

Best Guess
for *hyper-* at the beginning of a word = /hī pər/

Look at each word below. What sounds do you expect *de-*, *ex-*, and *hyper-* to stand for? The Best Guess is the right guess. Read the words.

debate	defend	except	expedition	extra
decision	degrade	excite	experiment	hypersensitive
declare	demolish	exclude	explain	hypertension
deduction	exceed	exercise	express	hyperventilate

In these words below, the second best guess for *de-* is correct.

debate   decompose   decongestant   deodorize   desegregate

Find four words below in which *ex-* is followed by a vowel. The second best guess for *ex-* helps you say these four words.

extinct   exaggerate   exam   experience   exist   exult

Read all the words aloud. Listen for the sound of each prefix.

Go on to the next page.

Now read these sentences. If you have trouble with a word, try a different sound.

1. He became so <u>excited</u>, he began to <u>hyperventilate</u>.

2. The scientist did not <u>expect</u> the <u>experiment</u> to <u>demolish</u> his lab.

3. <u>Hyperactive</u> children tend to <u>exhaust</u> me.

4. This <u>decongestant</u> should help <u>defeat</u> your cold <u>extra</u> quickly.

5. I'd like to <u>examine</u> the facts before making my <u>decision</u>.

(Extra Practice, p. 199)

Word Beginnings *il-*, *im-*, *in-*, and *ir-*

/il/ illegal /im/ imbalance /in/ incomplete /ir/ irregular

When *il-*, *im-*, *in-*, or *ir-* comes at the beginning of a word, it probably has the short *i* sound followed by the sound for the consonant *l*, *m*, *n*, or *r*. Say the words *illegal*, *imbalance*, *incomplete*, and *irregular*. Can you hear the /il/, /im/, /in/, and /ir/ sounds at the beginnings of these words?

Best Guess

for *il-*, *im-*, *in-*, or *ir-* at the beginning of a word = /il/, /im/, /in/, or /ir/

Find four words that begin with the prefix *in-*. Say the words.

idol   incapable   itch   insane   invalidate   ignore   incurable

Look at the words below. Look at the beginning of each word. What sound do you expect *il-*, *im-*, *in-*, or *ir-* to stand for at the beginning of each word? The Best Guess helps you say these words correctly. Now read the words.

illegal	imitate	imperfect	informal	irrational
illegible	immature	impolite	initial	irreconcilable
illegitimate	immeasurable	inane	innocent	irregular
illiterate	immobile	incredible	insensible	irrelevance
illusion	impartial	indefinite	invaluable	irresistible

Read all the words aloud. Listen for the sound at the beginning of each word.

Now read these sentences. Notice the beginning of each underlined word.

1. They will <u>investigate</u> the <u>irregular</u> habits of the <u>illustrious</u> actor.

2. He is an <u>immature</u>, <u>impolite</u>, <u>illogical</u>, and <u>irritating</u> person.

3. Her <u>illegible</u> handwriting <u>infuriated</u> her boss.

4. I find it <u>incredible</u> that the damage to my car is <u>irreparable</u>.

5. <u>Invaluable</u> advice saved me an <u>immeasurable</u> amount of work.

(Extra Practice, p. 200)

Word Beginnings *mega-*, *micro-*, and *mini-*

/meg ə/ megaphone /mī krō/ microwave
/mī krə/ microscope /min ē/ minibike /min ə/ minimal

When *mega-* comes at the beginning of a word, it usually stands for the /meg ə/ sound heard at the beginning of *megaphone*. When *micro-* comes at the beginning of a word, it sometimes has the /mī krō/ sound that you hear in *microwave*. It can also stand for the /mī krə/ sound heard at the beginning of *microscope*. When *mini-* comes at the beginning of a word, it may stand for the /min ē/ sound heard in *minibike* or the /min ə/ sound heard in *minimal*. Say the key words to yourself and listen for the beginning sounds.

Best Guess
for *mega-* at the beginning of a word = /meg ə/

Best Guess
for *micro-* at the beginning of a word = /mī krō/
Second best guess = /mī krə/

Best Guess
for *mini-* at the beginning of a word = /min ē/
Second best guess = /min ə/

Look at the words below. What sound do you expect *mega-*, *micro-*, or *mini-* to stand for at the beginning of each word? The Best Guess is the right guess. Now read the words.

megabyte	megawatt	microcosm	miniature	minicar
megadose	microbe	microfilm	minibus	minicomputer
megavitamin	microbiology	microorganism	minicam	miniskirt

In these words below, the second best guesses are correct.

microphone microscopic microspore minimize minimum minister

Read all the words aloud. Listen for the sound at the beginning of each word.

Now read these sentences. Notice the beginning of each underlined word.

1. The library has *The New York Times* on microfilm.

2. How many megabytes of memory does your minicomputer have?

3. A microorganism can be seen only with a microscope.

4. To minimize fatigue, the doctor prescribed megavitamins for Ed.

5. Our office is a microcosm of the larger surrounding community.

(Extra Practice, p. 200)

Word Beginnings *non-* and *per-*

/non/ nonfiction   /pər/ permission   /pėr/ permanent

The prefix *non-* usually has the /non/ sound and stands for one syllable, as in *nonfiction*. The word beginning *per-* usually has the /pər/ sound heard in *permission*. In stressed syllables, *per-* may also stand for the /pėr/ sound heard in *permanent*. It may be difficult to hear the difference between these two sounds for *per-*.

Best Guess
for *non-* at the beginning of a word = /non/
for *per-* at the beginning of a word = /pər/ or /pėr/

Look at each word below. What sound do you expect *non-* or *per-* to stand for at the beginning of each word? Now read the words.

nonabsorbent	nonexistent	nonprofit	perfection	perplexity
nonaddictive	nonfattening	nonviolence	perform	personify
nonbreakable	nonnegotiable	perceive	perfume	perspective
nonchalant	nonpayment	percentage	perpetual	persuade

In these words, *per-* is a stressed syllable. Read the words.

percolate	perjury	permeate	persecute	personal
perforate	perky	perpetrate	persevere	pertinent

Read all the words aloud. Listen for the sound at the beginning of each word.

Now read these sentences. Notice the beginning of each underlined word.

1. This letter <u>pertains</u> to the <u>nonpayment</u> of your bill.

2. The conditions of this contract are <u>nonnegotiable</u>.

3. Jay has a <u>perplexing personality</u> that is difficult to <u>perceive</u>.

4. I assure you that this dessert is <u>nonfattening</u>.

5. He <u>perpetrated</u> a series of <u>nonviolent</u> crimes in our town.

(Extra Practice, p. 201)

— EXCEPTIONS —

peril (per'əl)   period (pir'ē əd)   periscope (per'ə skōp)

Word Beginnings *poly-* and *post-*
/pol ē/ polygon /pōst/ postpone

When the letters *poly-* come at the beginning of a word, they usually stand for the /pol ē/ sound heard in *polygon*. Most words that begin with the letters *post-* have the /pōst/ sound heard in *postpone*.

Best Guess
for *poly-* at the beginning of a word = /pol ē/
for *post-* at the beginning of a word = /pōst/

Look at the words below. Look at the beginning of each word. What sound do you expect *poly-* or *post-* to stand for at the beginning of each word? Now read the words.

polyester	polystyrene	polyvinyl	poster	postnasal
polyethylene	polyunsaturated	postage	postmaster	postpone
polyphonic	polyurethane	postdate	postmortem	postscript

Read all the words aloud. Listen for the sound at the beginning of each word.

Now read these sentences. Notice the beginning of each underlined word.

1. A <u>polyester</u> shirt won't shrink the way a cotton shirt will.

2. We will <u>postpone</u> the lecture if the snow continues.

3. The corn oil I use is <u>polyunsaturated</u>.

4. We use <u>polyethylene</u> to cover the gas grill in the winter.

5. How much <u>postage</u> did you pay to mail that <u>poster</u>?

(Extra Practice, p. 201)

— EXCEPTIONS —

polygamy (pə lig′ə mē)
polymer (pol′ə mər)
polynesia (pol′ə nē′zhə)

posterity (po ster′ə tē)
posthumous (pos′chə məs)
posture (pos′chər)

115

Word Beginnings *pre-* and *pro-*

/pri/ prepare   /prē/ prearrange   /pre/ prejudice
/prǝ/ promote   /prō/ program   /pro/ promise

When *pre-* comes at the beginning of a word, it usually has one of three sounds. It may stand for the /pri/ sound heard in *prepare*. It may have the /prē/ sound heard in *prearrange*. It may also have the /pre/ sound you hear in *prejudice*. When *pro-* comes at the beginning of a word, it may stand for the /prǝ/ sound heard in *promote*. It may also stand for the /prō/ sound in *program* or the /pro/ sound in *promise*. The best way to determine which sounds *pre-* and *pro-* have is to try a sound. If you do not recognize the word, try another sound.

Best Guess
for *pre-* at the beginning of a word = /pri/
Second best guess = /prē/
Third best guess = /pre/

Best Guess
for *pro-* at the beginning of a word = /prǝ/
Second best guess = /prō/
Third best guess = /pro/

Look at each word below. What sound do you expect *pre-* to stand for at the beginning of each word? The Best Guess is the right guess. Now read the words.

precaution	preclude	prefer	prescribe	presumption
precipitate	predicament	preliminary	prescription	prevail
precise	predictable	prepare	preservative	prevent

The second best guess is the right guess for the words below.

preamble	preconception	predigest	prefix	premature
precede	predate	preexist	prejudge	prerecord

Try the third best guess to read these *pre-* words.

predator	preface	prelude	premise	preparation

Read all the words aloud. Listen for the sound at the beginning of each word.

Now read these sentences. If you have trouble with a word, try a different sound at the beginning.

1. It is probably premature to begin preparations for the party.
2. We took preliminary precautions to preserve the land.
3. It was predictable that she would arrive precisely on time.
4. They learned about prepositions and prefixes in English class.
5. Preexisting conditions prevented us from presenting the play.

Look at each word below. What sound do you expect *pro-* to stand for? The Best Guess is the right guess. Now read the words.

proceed	profane	profound	promote	proportion
proclaim	profession	projection	pronounce	protect
production	professor	prolong	propeller	provide

The second best guess is the right guess for the words below.

probation	profile	pronoun	proscription	protocol
procrastinate	prohibit	propane	protest	protrude

Try the third best guess to read these *pro-* words.

probable	profit	prominent	prophesy	proposition

___ ___

Read all the words aloud. Listen for the sound at the beginning of each word.

Now read these sentences. If you have trouble with a word, try a different sound at the beginning.

1. It is probably a poor idea to ask for a promotion right now.
2. We can take more progressive measures to protect wildlife.
3. I couldn't promise Lena that I would join the protest.
4. If you procrastinate much longer, you may provoke the boss.
5. We will proceed to project our profits for next year.

(Extra Practice, p. 202)

Word Beginning *re-*

/rē/ reappear   /ri/ recover   /re/ recommend

The prefix *re-* stands for one syllable and usually has the /rē/ sound heard in *reappear*. The letters *re-* can often stand for the /ri/ sound that you hear at the beginning of *recover*. Sometimes *re-* has the /re/ sound heard in *recommend*.

Best Guess
for *re-* at the beginning of a word = /rē/
Second best guess = /ri/
Third best guess = /re/

Look at each word below. What sound do you expect *re-* to stand for? The Best Guess is the right guess. Now read the words.

reaffirm	redefine	refinance	remodel	reseal
reapply	redraw	regional	reopen	restructure
reclassify	reenact	reinterpret	reproduce	retype
reconvene	reevaluate	reload	reschedule	revitalize

In the words below, the second best guess is correct.

recall	reduce	rehearse	remember	return
receive	reflect	religion	request	review
recorder	refrigerate	remain	reside	reward

Try the third best guess to read these words that begin with *re-*.

reckless	reconcile	register	repetition	resignation
recollect	recreation	relative	reservation	restoration

Read all the words aloud. Listen for the sound of the letters *re-*.

Now read these sentences. If you have trouble with a word, try a different sound for the vowel *e* in the prefix.

1. I <u>recommend</u> that you <u>reduce</u> your price and <u>resubmit</u> the offer.

2. The town will <u>repave</u> our road and <u>repair</u> the sidewalks.

3. I don't <u>recall</u> the name of the hotel where I made <u>reservations</u>.

4. The doctor <u>requested</u> that I <u>reschedule</u> my appointment.

(Extra Practice, p. 202)

Word Beginnings *sub-*, *super-*, and *syn-*

**/sub/ subway /səb/ submerge /sü pər/ superman
/sin/ synonym**

When the prefix *sub-* begins a word, it stands for one syllable and usually has the /sub/ sound heard in *subway*. When the second syllable of the word is stressed, *sub-* usually stands for the /səb/ sound, as in *submerge*. It may be difficult to hear the difference between these two sounds.

The prefix *super-* usually stands for the /sü pər/ sound heard in *superman*. The prefix *syn-* has the /sin/ sound heard in *synonym*.

Best Guess
for *sub-* at the beginning of a word = /sub/
Second best guess = /səb/

Best Guess
for *super-* at the beginning of a word = /sü pər/
for *syn-* at the beginning of a word = /sin/

Look at each word below. What sound do you expect *sub-*, *super-*, or *syn-* to stand for at the beginning of each word? The Best Guess is the right guess. Now read the words.

subculture	substandard	supercool	supersede	synonym
subdivide	substitute	superficial	supervisor	synopsis
sublet	subtitle	superhuman	synagogue	synthesizer
submarine	supercharge	supermarket	syndicate	synthetic

In the words below, the second best guess for *sub-* is the right guess.

subdue	submerge	subordinate	subsist	suburban
sublime	submit	subside	subtract	subversive

Read all the words aloud. Listen for the stressed syllable in each word.

Take a look at the sentences on the next page.

Now read these sentences. Notice the beginning of each underlined word.

1. It is difficult to <u>subsist</u> on a <u>substandard</u> salary.

2. I attend the <u>synagogue</u> near the new <u>supermarket</u>.

3. His <u>syndicated</u> column is popular with the <u>subculture</u>.

4. She presented the <u>synopsis</u> of the book in a <u>subdued</u> voice.

5. The movie's <u>subtitle</u> was <u>superimposed</u> over the opening scene.

(Extra Practice, p. 203)

——EXCEPTIONS——

subpoena (sə pē′nə)   superior (sə pir′ē ər)

superfluous (sù per′flü əs)   superlative (sə pèr′lə tiv)

The word *subject* may be pronounced (sub′jikt) or (səb jekt′).

Word Beginnings *un-*, *uni-*, and *tele-*

/un/ uncooked   /yü nə/ unicycle   /tel ə/ telephone

The prefix *un-* stands for one syllable and often has the /un/ sound heard at the beginning of *uncooked*. The letters *uni-* stand for two syllables and often have the /yü nə/ sound heard in *unicycle*. Sometimes the prefix *un-* is added to a word that begins with the vowel *i*. When you see a word such as *unimportant*, try the /un/ sound and then the /yü nə/ sound to see which beginning sounds familiar. Generally, the letters *tele-* stand for the /tel ə/ sound heard in *telephone*.

Best Guess
for *un-* at the beginning of a word = /un/
for *uni-* at the beginning of a word = /yü nə/
for *tele-* at the beginning of a word = /tel ə/

Find three words in which the prefix *un-* is added to a word that begins with the vowel *i*. Say the words.

unimaginable   unmask   uninterrupted   unfasten   uninjured

Look at each word below. What sound do you expect *un-*, *uni-*, or *tele-* to stand for at the beginning of each word? Now read the words.

telecast	television	unclaimed	uniform	university
telegram	unafraid	unclear	uninformed	unmistaken
telescope	unassisted	undetermined	unisex	unproductive
telethon	uncalled	unharmed	universal	unsatisfying

———— 👂 ————

Read all the words aloud. Listen for the beginning sounds.

Now read these sentences. Notice the beginning of each underlined word.

1. Our basketball <u>uniforms</u> are <u>unshrinkable</u>.

2. The <u>university</u> graduation ceremony was <u>televised</u> locally.

3. The stolen <u>telescope</u> was <u>uninsured</u>.

4. The hospital <u>telecast</u> a <u>universal</u> appeal for a liver donor.

(Extra Practice, p. 203)

——— EXCEPTIONS ———

unique (yü nēk′)   united (yü nī′tid)

Word Endings -*able* and -*ible*

/ə bəl/ adorable, possible

The endings -*able* and -*ible* are usually said the same way. These endings can be divided into two syllables -*a/ble* and -*i/ble*. The vowel in each syllable generally has the schwa sound. Can you hear the /ə bəl/ sound at the ends of the words *adorable* and *possible*? Notice which syllables get the stress in these words.

Best Guess
for -*able* or -*ible* at the end of a word = /ə bəl/

Look at the list of words below. Look at each ending. What sound do you expect the ending -*able* or -*ible* to stand for at the end of each word? Now read the words.

acceptable	convertible	incredible	probable	sensible
affordable	dependable	invisible	profitable	shrinkable
agreeable	edible	irritable	questionable	terrible
believable	eligible	knowledgeable	reasonable	tolerable
breakable	favorable	likable	refundable	unreliable
capable	gullible	lovable	reliable	visible
comfortable	horrible	miserable	responsible	washable

Read all the words aloud. Listen for the stressed syllables in the words and for the schwa sounds in the endings.

Now read these sentences. Notice the ending in each underlined word.

1. Some wild mushrooms are <u>edible</u> while others are <u>inedible</u>.

2. If you purchase that sweater on sale, your money is <u>nonrefundable</u>.

3. Old dolls and rare stamps are <u>valuable</u> and <u>collectible</u>.

4. It is <u>unimaginable</u> that anyone could be so <u>gullible</u>.

5. Some people believe that all politicians are <u>corruptible</u>.

(Extra Practice, p. 204)

Word Endings Vowel + *cy* and Vowel + *sy*

/ə sē/   privacy, fantasy

When a word ends in a vowel followed by the letters *cy* or *sy*, the vowel usually has the schwa sound, and the *cy* or *sy* usually has the /sē/ sound. Say the words *privacy* and *fantasy*. Can you hear the /ə sē/ sound that the letters -*acy* and -*asy* stand for at the ends of the words?

Best Guess
for a vowel followed by *cy* or *sy* at the end of a word = /ə sē/

Look at the endings in these words. Which words end in a vowel followed by *cy*? How many words end in a vowel followed by *sy*? The Best Guess helps you say these words.

policy   heresy   ecstasy   legacy

Look at the list of words below. What sound do you expect at the end of each word? Now read the words.

accuracy	democracy	fantasy	immediacy	literacy
aristocracy	diplomacy	hypocrisy	legacy	pleurisy
celibacy	fallacy	illiteracy	legitimacy	supremacy

Read all the words aloud. Listen for the /ə sē/ sound in each ending. Notice which syllable in each word gets the stress.

Now read these sentences. Notice the ending in each underlined word.

1. Always check over your written work for <u>accuracy</u>.

2. The story of the talking horse was an example of a <u>fantasy</u>.

3. I make it a <u>policy</u> always to arrive on time for an appointment.

4. It was pure <u>idiocy</u> to enter the jungle without a guide.

5. In a <u>democracy</u>, every citizen has the right to vote.

(Extra Practice, p. 204)

Word Ending -*age*
/ij/ garbage /äzh/ garage

The ending -*age* often has the /ij/ sound. When you say the word *garbage* out loud, you can hear the /ij/ sound at the end of the word. Sometimes, the ending -*age* has the /äzh/ sound. Say the word *garage*. Can you hear the /äzh/ sound at the end?

Best Guess
for -*age* at the end of a word = /ij/
Second best guess = /äzh/

Look at the list of words below. Look at each ending. What sound do you expect -*age* to stand for at the end of each word? The Best Guess is the right guess. Now read the words.

advantage	cottage	foliage	message	shortage
average	courage	luggage	package	storage
baggage	damage	manage	passage	usage
bandage	dosage	marriage	postage	village

In the words below, the second best guess is correct. Read the words.

barrage	collage	corsage	massage	mirage

Read all the words aloud. Listen for the sound of the ending -*age*.

Now read these sentences. If you have trouble with a word, try a different sound for the -*age* ending.

1. We will <u>average</u> 25 miles a day on our bike trip.

2. They traveled to New England to see the fall <u>foliage</u>.

3. I left a <u>message</u> on Al's answering machine.

4. It took a lot of <u>courage</u> to face that angry crowd.

5. Ed pinned the <u>corsage</u> onto Maria's gown.

(Extra Practice, p. 205)

--- EXCEPTION ---

engage (en gāj´)

Word Endings -*ance* and -*ence*

/əns/ ambulance, difference

The word endings -*ance* and -*ence* usually stand for the /əns/ sound heard in *ambulance* and *difference*. Can you hear the /əns/ sound at the end of each word? Notice that the ending syllable does not get the most stress.

Best Guess
for -*ance* or -*ence* at the end of a word = /əns/

Look at the list of words below. Look at each ending. What sound do you expect the ending -*ance* or -*ence* to stand for at the end of each word? Now read the words.

acceptance	appearance	coincidence	excellence	persistence
absence	appliance	confidence	instance	radiance
admittance	balance	distance	intelligence	relevance
allowance	clearance	elegance	obedience	tolerance

Read the middle three columns of words aloud. Do the endings sound alike even though some words end with -*ance* and some end with -*ence*? Listen for the schwa sound in each ending.

Now read these sentences. Notice the ending in each underlined word.

1. She tries to <u>balance</u> the time between work and relaxation.

2. What a nice <u>coincidence</u> that we met you here today!

3. Do you know the <u>distance</u> between Boston and Montreal?

4. You will need a ticket to gain <u>admittance</u> to the concert.

5. I can't tell the <u>difference</u> between her twin daughters.

(Extra Practice, p. 205)

EXCEPTIONS

circumstance (sėr′kəm stans)   commence (kə mens′)

Word Endings -*ant* and -*ent*

/ənt/ important, excellent

The endings -*ant* and -*ent* usually stand for the /ənt/ sound heard at the end of *important* and *excellent*. When -*ant* and -*ent* follow the vowel *i*, as in the word *obedient*, the *i* often has the long *e* sound. Sometimes, -*iant* or -*ient* sounds like /yənt/, as in *convenient*.

Best Guess
for -*ant* or -*ent* at the end of a word = /ənt/

Best Guess
for -*iant* and -*ient* at the end of a word = /ē ənt/
Second best guess = /yənt/

Look at the list of words below. Do any of the endings follow the vowel *i*? In all these words, the Best Guesses are right. Now read the words.

applicant	dependent	ignorant	obedient	resident
assistant	deviant	important	radiant	urgent
confident	different	independent	recent	violent
consistent	excellent	intelligent	remnant	warrant

In the words below, the second best guess for -*iant* and -*ient* is correct.

brilliant	convenient	valiant

Read all the words aloud. Can you hear the schwa sound in each ending?

Now read the sentences. If you have trouble with words that have the vowel *i* before the ending, try a different sound.

1. Tom is the <u>assistant</u> manager at the <u>department</u> store.

2. The police could not enter the <u>apartment</u> without a <u>warrant</u>.

3. It is <u>apparent</u> that you are an <u>excellent</u> cook.

4. A <u>radiant</u> sun was shining down on fields of flowers.

5. He is a <u>current</u> <u>resident</u> of this country.

(Extra Practice, p. 206)

EXCEPTIONS

defiant (di fī'ənt)   reliant (ri lī'ənt)

Word Ending -*ate*

/āt/ locate   /it/ pirate

The ending -*ate* often stands for the /āt/ sound heard at the end of *locate*. Sometimes, -*ate* at the end of a word has the /it/ sound, as in *pirate*.

Best Guess
for -*ate* at the end of a word = /āt/
Second best guess = /it/

Look at the list of words below. What sound do you expect -*ate* to stand for at the end of each word? In all these words, the Best Guess is the right guess. Now read the words.

accommodate	dictate	exaggerate	implicate	relate
celebrate	donate	fabricate	investigate	tolerate
communicate	elevate	hallucinate	narrate	translate
decorate	equate	imitate	navigate	violate

In the words below, the second best guess is correct.

adequate	considerate	illiterate	literate	pirate
compassionate	corporate	inanimate	passionate	surrogate

Read all the words aloud. Listen for the sound of -*ate*.

Now read these sentences. If you have trouble with a word, try a different sound for the ending.

1. The small restaurant could not <u>accommodate</u> our large group.
2. He wishes to <u>donate</u> a large sum of money to charity.
3. The company's <u>corporate</u> headquarters are in Buffalo, New York.
4. You will feel better if you sit and <u>elevate</u> your feet for a while.
5. Tim is a loving and <u>compassionate</u> father.

(Extra Practice, p. 206)

---EXCEPTIONS---

The word *appropriate* may be pronounced (ə prō′prē it) or (ə prō′prē āt). The word *separate* may be pronounced (sep′ə rāt′) or (sep′ər it).

Word Ending -*ed*

/ed/ hunted /d/ begged /t/ walked

When -*ed* is added to a word that ends in *d* or *t*, the -*ed* ending often stands for the /ed/ sound heard in *hunted*. When -*ed* is added to a word that does not end in *d* or *t*, the *e* is silent. Then the -*ed* ending usually sounds like /d/ or /t/. Say the word *begged*. Can you hear the /d/ sound at the end? Now say *walked*. Do you hear the /t/ sound at the end?

Best Guess
for -*ed* following *d* or *t* at the end of a word = /ed/
for -*ed* following other letters at the end of a word = /d/ or /t/

Find four words in which -*ed* does <u>not</u> follow a *d* or *t*. Say the words.

tested   forced   bumped   added   kicked   looked

Look at the list of words below. What letter comes before the -*ed* ending? What sound do you expect -*ed* to stand for? Now read the words.

added	ended	hoped	pinched	shredded
aided	filled	injected	relented	treated
danced	granted	melted	risked	vanished

Read all the words aloud. Listen for the sound of the last syllable of each word.

Now read these sentences. Notice the letter that comes before the -*ed* ending in each underlined word.

1. The doctor <u>injected</u> his patient with a pain-killing medicine.

2. I <u>added</u> up the column of numbers and <u>checked</u> my addition twice.

3. We <u>danced</u> until the music <u>ended</u> at midnight.

4. When the snow <u>melted</u>, we <u>walked</u> home through the slush.

5. That machine <u>shredded</u> all the secret papers he had <u>saved</u>.

(Extra Practice, p. 207)

— EXCEPTIONS —

jagged (jag′id)   naked (nā′kid)   wicked (wik′id)

Word Ending -*ine*

/ēn/ machine   /ən/ imagine

The ending -*ine* usually stands for the /ēn/ sound heard in *machine*.
Sometimes -*ine* at the end of a word has the /ən/ sound, as in *imagine*.

Best Guess
for -*ine* at the end of a word = /ēn/
Second best guess = /ən/

Look at the list of words below. What sound do you expect -*ine* to stand
for at the end of each word? In all these words, the Best Guess is the
right guess. Now read the words.

amphetamine	Christine	magazine	quarantine	routine
chlorine	machine	marine	morphine	saline

In the words below, the second best guess is correct. Read the words.

determine	examine	imagine	margarine	medicine

Read all the words aloud. Listen for the /ēn/ or /ən/ sound at the end
of each word.

Now read these sentences. If you have trouble reading a word, try
saying the ending with a different sound.

1. Can you <u>imagine</u> what it would be like to be the president?

2. <u>Amphetamines</u> are <u>medicine</u> and should be given by a doctor.

3. John added <u>chlorine</u> to the swimming pool water.

4. This <u>margarine</u> has less fat than butter has.

5. Pam's exercise <u>routine</u> included running five miles every day.

(Extra Practice, p. 207)

— EXCEPTION —

asinine (as'n īn)

Word Endings -*ism* and -*asm*

/iz əm/ communism   /az əm/ sarcasm

When you see -*ism* or -*asm* at the end of a word, it may help if you divide the ending into two syllables. The *s* in the first syllable of each ending usually has the /z/ sound. The second syllable usually has the sound /əm/. Say the words *communism* and *sarcasm*. Can you hear the sound of /iz əm/ at the end of *communism*? Can you hear the sound of /az əm/ at the end of *sarcasm*?

Best Guess
for -*ism* at the end of a word = /iz əm/
for -*asm* at the end of a word = /az əm/

Look at the list of words below. What sound do you expect the -*ism* or -*asm* to stand for at the end of each word? Now read the words.

alcoholism	chasm	humanism	optimism	racism
baptism	commercialism	idealism	patriotism	realism
Buddhism	criticism	mannerism	pessimism	sarcasm
capitalism	cynicism	mechanism	plagiarism	spasm
Catholicism	enthusiasm	mysticism	Protestantism	symbolism

Read all the words aloud. Listen for the /iz əm/ or /az əm/ sound in each ending.

Now read these sentences. Notice the ending in each underlined word.

1. The angry young man replied with <u>cynicism</u> and <u>sarcasm</u>.

2. <u>Alcoholism</u> is a treatable disease.

3. <u>Materialism</u> and <u>capitalism</u> may go hand-in-hand.

4. She took medicine for painful muscle <u>spasms</u> in her back.

5. He showed <u>optimism</u>, believing he could leap over the <u>chasm</u>.

(Extra Practice, p. 208)

Word Endings -*ity* and -*ety*

/ə tē/ unity, society

When a word ends in *i* or *e* followed by the letters *ty*, the vowel usually has the schwa sound, and the *ty* usually has the /tē/ sound. Say the words *unity* and *society*. Can you hear the /ə tē/ sound that -*ity* and -*ety* stand for at the ends of the words?

Best Guess
for -*ity* or -*ety* at the end of a word = /ə tē/

Look at the words below. Which words end in -*ity*? Find the word that ends in -*ety*. The Best Guess helps you say all these words.

| sanity | ability | nicety | charity |

Now look at the words below. What sound do you expect the ending to stand for in each word? Read the words.

anxiety	disability	hostility	notoriety	sincerity
capacity	entirety	identity	personality	sobriety
celebrity	electricity	immunity	possibility	society
clarity	facility	liability	propriety	university
community	futility	morality	quantity	variety
curiosity	gravity	necessity	security	vulgarity

Read all the words aloud. Listen for the /ə tē/ sound in each ending. Notice that the sound is the same whether the ending is spelled with -*ity* or -*ety*.

Now read the sentences. Notice the ending in each underlined word.

1. Although he was a big <u>celebrity</u>, he spoke with real <u>sincerity</u>.
2. Does everyone in our <u>society</u> share the same <u>quality</u> of life?
3. There are a <u>variety</u> of activities at the <u>community</u> center.
4. Reverend Thomas spoke with <u>sanctity</u> and <u>piety</u>.
5. The <u>university</u> will have to close in its <u>entirety</u>.

(Extra Practice, p. 208)

131

Word Ending -*ive*

/iv/ active /īv/ arrive

When the ending -*ive* follows the letter *s* or *t* in a word, it usually has the /iv/ sound heard in *active*. When the letters -*ive* do not follow an *s* or a *t*, they usually follow the VCV pattern and stand for the /īv/ sound heard in *arrive*.

Best Guess
for -*ive* following *s* or *t* at the end of a word = /iv/
for -*ive* following other letters at the end of a word = /īv/

Look at the words below. What letter does the -*ive* ending follow in each word? What sound do you expect the ending to stand for? Now read the words.

active	defensive	incentive	legislative	receptive
automotive	distinctive	indicative	narrative	relative
competitive	elective	informative	progressive	selective
creative	extensive	instructive	provocative	tentative

In the words below, the ending does not follow an *s* or a *t*. Read the words.

alive	contrive	derive	survive	revive

Read all the words aloud. Listen for the sound at the end of each word.

Now read these sentences. Notice the letter that comes before the -*ive* ending in each underlined word.

1. He learned to do <u>extensive</u> car repairs in an <u>automotive</u> class.

2. You may <u>revive</u> your <u>creative</u> powers with rest.

3. I have a <u>relative</u> who is very <u>active</u> and <u>competitive</u> in sports.

4. What <u>motive</u> did she have, telling such a <u>provocative</u> <u>narrative</u>?

5. We have an <u>instinctive</u> nature to <u>survive</u> and stay <u>alive</u>.

(Extra Practice, p. 209)

Word Ending -*le*

/əl/ circle   /l/ little

The ending -*le* usually has the /əl/ sound heard at the end of *circle*. When -*le* follows *dd* or *tt*, -*le* often sounds like the letter *l* only. It may be difficult to hear the difference between these two sounds.

Best Guess
for -*le* at the end of a word = /əl/
for -*le* following *dd* or *tt* at the end of a word = /l/

Look at the words below. Look at each ending. What sound do you expect the ending -*le* to stand for in each word? Read the words.

able	couple	huddle	needle	scribble
angle	dimple	idle	noodle	simple
Bible	dribble	jungle	people	table
bottle	fiddle	kettle	pimple	trouble
bubble	gentle	ladle	puddle	uncle
buckle	giggle	middle	rattle	whittle

Read the first two columns of words aloud. Listen for the /əl/ or /l/ sound at the end of each word.

Now read these sentences. Notice that some words end in -*led*. It is important to keep the /əl/ sound in these words. Listen for the /əld/ sound at the end of these words.

1. The little girl giggled when the purple bubble broke.

2. She scribbled a simple design in the middle of the paper.

3. Water will dribble from the kettle and make a puddle.

4. The jumble of books tumbled from the table.

5. Wax will trickle down the side of the candle.

(Extra Practice, p. 209)

Word Ending -*ous*

/əs/ famous

The word ending -*ous* has the /əs/ sound heard at the end of *famous*. Usually, when a word ends in *i* or *e* followed by the -*ous* ending, the *i* or *e* has the long *e* sound heard in *previous*. When -*ous* follows *gi* or *ge*, you often hear the /jəs/ sound. Say the word *contagious*. Can you hear the /jəs/ sound at the end? A few words end in *u* followed by -*ous*. These words have the /yü əs/ sound heard at the end of *continuous*.

Best Guess
for -*ous* at the end of a word = /əs/
for -*ous* following *i* or *e* at the end of a word = /ē əs/
for -*ous* following *gi* or *ge* at the end of a word = /jəs/
for -*ous* following *u* at the end of a word = /yü əs/

Look at the words below. What letters come before -*ous*? What sound do you expect -*ous* to stand for at the end of each word? Now read the words.

beauteous	delirious	hilarious	marvelous	prosperous
contagious	furious	instantaneous	miscellaneous	religious
courageous	generous	jealous	numerous	serious
curious	gorgeous	joyous	perilous	strenuous
dangerous	hideous	luminous	poisonous	various

Read all the words aloud. Listen for the /əs/ sound in each ending.

Now read these sentences. Notice the letters that come before the -*ous* endings in the underlined words.

1. The child's birth was a <u>wondrous</u> and <u>joyous</u> event.

2. In his <u>previous</u> job, he had <u>miscellaneous</u> <u>tedious</u> tasks.

3. It's <u>dangerous</u> to do such <u>strenuous</u> work on a <u>continuous</u> basis.

4. She was <u>courageous</u> to climb that <u>perilous</u> mountain.

5. It was <u>obvious</u> that his answer was <u>erroneous</u>.

(Extra Practice, p. 210)

Word Endings -*sure* and -*sual*

/zhər/ pleasure   /shər/ pressure   /zhü əl/ usual
/shü əl/ sensual

When the letter *s* is followed by -*ure* or -*ual* at the end of a word, the *s* often stands for the /zh/ sound. Can you hear the /zhər/ sound at the end of *pleasure*? Can you hear the /zhü əl/ sound at the end of *usual*? The letter *s* can also have the /sh/ sound heard in *pressure*.

Best Guess
for -*sure* at the end of a word = /zhər/
Second best guess = /shər/

Best Guess
for -*sual* at the end of a word = /zhü əl/
Second best guess = /shü əl/

Look at each word below. What sound do you expect the *s* to stand for in each ending? In all these words, the Best Guesses are the right guesses. Now read the words.

casual	composure	exposure	measure	unusual
closure	enclosure	leisure	treasure	visual

In the words below, the second best guesses are correct.

assure	fissure	insure	reassure	sensual

Read all the words aloud. Listen for the sound that *s* stands for in each word.

Now read these sentences. If you have trouble reading a word, try saying the *s* with a different sound.

1. We take a casual walk whenever we have some leisure time.

2. I can assure you that she is behaving in an unusual way.

3. He made a public disclosure about the hidden treasure.

4. The actress has a sensual way of moving and talking.

5. Lin is able to keep her composure even under pressure.

(Extra Practice, p. 210)

Word Endings -*tion* and -*ssion*

/shən/ nation, passion

The word endings -*tion* and -*ssion* usually have the /shən/ sound. Say the words *nation* and *passion*. Can you hear the /shən/ sound at the end of each word?

Best Guess
for -*tion* or -*ssion* at the end of a word = /shən/

Look at the words below. What sound do you expect each ending -*tion* or -*ssion* to stand for at the end of each word? Read the words.

action	discussion	intuition	petition	succession
admission	edition	junction	recession	suction
caution	elevation	mission	repetition	traction
compassion	fraction	partition	sanitation	tradition
concession	graduation	perception	session	vacation
convention	injection	permission	station	verification

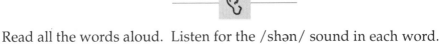

Read all the words aloud. Listen for the /shən/ sound in each word. Notice that the end sound is the same even when the endings are spelled differently.

Now read these sentences. Notice the ending in each underlined word.

1. There was a <u>procession</u> of students before the <u>graduation</u> ceremony.

2. Jon has an excellent <u>reputation</u> in his <u>profession</u>.

3. <u>Construction</u> of new homes usually slows during a <u>recession</u>.

4. Mary's <u>condition</u> has improved; her cancer is in <u>remission</u>.

5. What was his <u>reaction</u> to the prisoner's <u>confession</u>?

(Extra Practice, p. 211)

EXCEPTIONS

digestion (də jes'chən)   question (kwes'chən)

Word Ending -*sion*

/zhən/ vision   /shən/ tension

The ending -*sion* often stands for the /zhən/ sound heard in *vision*. Sometimes the ending -*sion* has the /shən/ sound. When you say the word *tension*, you can hear the sound of /shən/ at the end.

Best Guess
for -*sion* at the end of a word = /zhən/
Second best guess = /shən/

Look at the words below. What sound do you expect -*sion* to stand for at the end of each word? In all these words, the Best Guess is the right guess. Now read the words.

adhesion	conversion	exclusion	occasion	reversion
aversion	decision	excursion	perversion	revision
collision	diversion	fusion	precision	television
confusion	division	incision	provision	version

In the words below, the second best guess is correct. Read the words.

apprehension	compulsion	expulsion	pension	suspension
comprehension	dimension	extension	propulsion	tension

Read all the words aloud. Listen for the sound of -*sion*. In which words do you hear the /zhən/ sound? In which words do you hear the /shən/ sound?

Now read these sentences. If you have trouble with a word, try a different sound for the ending.

1. I have no <u>comprehension</u> of what that <u>television</u> show was about.

2. After the <u>collision</u>, she had an <u>aversion</u> to driving at night.

3. The surgeon made the <u>incision</u> with <u>precision</u>.

4. They did not make a <u>provision</u> to pay the writer for <u>revisions</u>.

5. Carlo measured the <u>dimensions</u> of the doorway.

(Extra Practice, p. 211)

Endings after *ti-*, *ci-*, and *sci-*

/shəl/ partial   /shənt/ patient   /shən/ electrician
/shē āt/ appreciate   /shəns/ conscience   /shəs/ conscious

When the letters *ti*, *ci*, or *sci* appear before many word endings, they generally have the same /sh/ sound. This is true with the endings -*al*, -*an*, -*ate*, -*ent*, -*ence*, and -*ous*. Read the key words above and listen to the sound the letters *ti*, *ci*, and *sci* stand for in the words. Notice, too, that most of the endings have the schwa sound in them.

The letters -*tian* or -*cian* at the end of a word usually have the /shən/ sound heard in *Egyptian* and *electrician*. The letters -*tience* or -*science* at the end of a word usually have the /shəns/ sound heard in *patience* and *conscience*. The letters -*tient*, -*cient*, or -*scient* at the end of a word usually have the /shənt/ sound heard in *patient*, *sufficient*, and *omniscient*.

The letters -*tiate* or -*ciate* at the end of a word are different. They form two syllables and they do not have a schwa sound. Read the words *negotiate* and *appreciate*. Notice that the letters -*tiate* and -*ciate* stand for two syllables, /shē āt/.

Best Guess
for -*tian* or -*cian* at the end of a word = /shən/
for -*tience* or -*science* at the end of a word = /shəns/
for -*tient*, -*cient*, or -*scient* at the end of a word = /shənt/
for -*tiate* or -*ciate* at the end of a word = /shē āt/

Look at each word below and its ending. What sound do you expect to hear at the end of each word? Now read the words.

appreciate	differentiate	impatient	omniscience	pediatrician
conscience	efficient	magician	omniscient	physician
deficient	electrician	obstetrician	patience	technician
dietician	gentian	officiate	patient	Venetian

Read all the words aloud. Listen for the /sh/ sound for each ending.

Now read these sentences. Notice the *ti, ci,* and *sci* in the underlined words.

1. The doctor <u>appreciates</u> it when her <u>patients</u> arrive on time.
2. A <u>magician</u> entertained the children at the company picnic.
3. She ate <u>insufficiently</u> and suffered from a vitamin <u>deficiency</u>.
4. A guilty <u>conscience</u> forced the <u>politician</u> to confess the truth.
5. He will <u>negotiate</u> a contract for a <u>sufficient</u> amount of money.

The letters *ti* or *ci* have the /sh/ sound before the ending *-al.* Say the words *partial* and *financial.* Do you hear the /shəl/ sound at the end of both words?

The letters *ti, ci,* and *sci* usually have the /sh/ sound when they come before the ending *-ous.* Say the words *ambitious* and *conscious.* Do you hear the /shəs/ sound at the end of each word?

Best Guess
for *-tial* and *-cial* at the end of a word = /shəl/
for *-tious, -cious,* and *-scious* at the end of a word = /shəs/

Look at each word in the list below. Notice whether the ending *-al* follows *ti* or *ci.* What sound do you expect to hear at the end of each word? Now read the words.

beneficial	essential	judicial	residential	special
commercial	facial	partial	sequential	substantial
confidential	impartial	potential	social	superficial
crucial	initial	racial	spatial	torrential

Read the last two columns aloud. Listen for the /shəl/ sound in the endings. What letters spell the /shəl/ sound at the end of each word?

Now go on to the next page.

Look at each word in the list below. What sound do you expect to hear at the end of each word? Now read the words.

ambitious	fictitious	ostentatious	rambunctious	unconscious
atrocious	luscious	precious	scrumptious	vicious
cautious	malicious	precocious	superstitious	vivacious
ferocious	officious	pretentious	suspicious	voracious

Read all the words aloud. What letters stand for the /shəs/ sound at the end of each word?

Now read these sentences. Notice the ending in each underlined word.

1. You should be <u>cautious</u> when driving in a <u>residential</u> area.

2. The senator is a <u>potential</u> <u>presidential</u> candidate.

3. It is <u>essential</u> that you apologize for your <u>atrocious</u> behavior.

4. The dinner <u>special</u> looks <u>scrumptious</u>.

5. The <u>ambitious</u> young woman received a <u>substantial</u> salary increase.

(Extra Practice, p. 212)

—— EXCEPTION ——

Christian (kris'chən)

Word Endings -*ture* and -*tual*

/chər/ nature   /chü əl/ actual

When the letter *t* is followed by -*ure* or -*ual* at the end of a word, the *t* often stands for the /ch/ sound. Say the words *nature* and *actual*. Can you hear the /chər/ sound at the end of *nature*? Can you hear the /chü əl/ sound at the end of *actual*?

Best Guess
for -*ture* at the end of a word = /chər/
for -*tual* at the end of a word = /chü əl/

Look at the words below. Look at each -*ture* and -*tual* ending. What sound do you expect the *t* to stand for in each word? Now read the words.

adventure	eventual	intellectual	perpetual	signature
architecture	factual	literature	picture	spiritual
conceptual	feature	miniature	punctual	texture
contractual	fracture	mixture	ritual	venture
culture	furniture	mutual	rupture	virtual
creature	gesture	perceptual	sculpture	vulture

Read all the words aloud. Listen for the sound that *t* stands for in each word. In which words do you hear the /chər/ sound? In which words do you hear the /chü əl/ sound?

Now read these sentences. Notice the ending in each underlined word.

1. We have a <u>mutual</u> appreciation of fine <u>literature</u>.

2. The <u>texture</u> of the fabric on her <u>furniture</u> was velvety smooth.

3. That story is a <u>mixture</u> of the <u>factual</u> and fictitious.

4. In the <u>future</u>, try to be <u>punctual</u> for your appointments.

5. It was a daily <u>ritual</u> for him to feed the woodland <u>creatures</u>.

(Extra Practice, p. 212)

— EXCEPTIONS —

The word *mature* may be pronounced (mə chúr'), (mə túr'), or (mə tyúr').

Mixed Review

Practice what you have learned by reading these sentences.

1. He has an irresistible personality.

2. Our conclusions were consistent with hers.

3. She regarded her reflection in the mirror.

4. His acceptance to the state university came on Tuesday.

5. I can't tolerate her pretentious mannerisms.

6. All nonessential personnel were encouraged to retire.

7. Nancy will illustrate an adorable children's book.

8. This nation needs to make a commitment to better education.

9. That young child shows unlimited enthusiasm for learning.

10. Carla bemoans the fact that she had refused to cooperate.

11. It's impolite to brag about your own level of intelligence.

12. His disability does not prevent him from being active.

13. Jay belongs to the Society of Automotive Mechanics.

14. The teacher demanded that the girl stop blowing bubbles.

15. Hypertension can be a dangerous condition.

16. The physician administered a megadose of antibiotics.

17. Lena is curious about life aboard a submarine.

18. Polyester is a synthetic fabric.

19. It was unusual for Joan to put pressure on her employees.

20. Joe probably stopped at the supermarket on his way home.

21. My conscience hounds me when I procrastinate.

22. I couldn't understand their discussion about microbiology.

23. Lynne values her privacy like a treasure.

24. Miniature doll house furniture is expensive.

25. You can't imagine how much money a telethon can raise.

Most words follow common rules that make them easier to read. However, there are many words that do not follow the rules. These words may have silent letters in them, unusual letter teams, or letters used in unusual ways.

There are many reasons words may be hard to read. One reason is that the English language uses words from other languages. Some of these words have changed their sounds over the years, but they have not changed their letter patterns.

Part 5 will teach you how to read many such words. Some you may know already. Look over the key words below to find out.

know	/n/	page 145	**gra**ph	/f/	page 149
gnaw	/n/	page 145	**p**sychic	/s/	page 150
pneumonia	/n/	page 145	**qu**ick	/kw/	page 151
write	/r/	page 145	s**qu**are	/kw/	page 151
rhyme	/r/	page 145	li**qu**or	/k/	page 151
li**s**ten	/s/	page 147	anti**que**	/k/	page 151
cli**mb**	/m/	page 147	**wh**ite	/hw/	page 152
autu**mn**	/m/	page 147	bo**x**	/ks/	page 153
fol**k**	/k/	page 147	te**x**t	/ks/	page 153
hour	/silent h/	page 147	obno**x**ious	/ksh/	page 153
physical	/f/	page 149	**x**ylophone	/z/	page 153
tele**ph**one	/f/	page 149	ball**et**	/ā/	page 154

Silent Letters in *kn*, *gn*, *pn*, *wr*, and *rh*

/n/ know, gnaw, pneumonia   /r/ write, rhyme

When the letters *kn*, *gn*, or *pn* come at the beginning of a word, they generally stand for the /n/ sound. Say the words *know*, *gnaw*, and *pneumonia*. Do you hear the /n/ sound at the beginning of those words? You don't hear the sounds for the letters *k*, *g*, and *p* because they are silent when they are followed by the letter *n* at the beginning of a word. When the letters *wr* or *rh* come at the beginning of a word, they stand for the /r/ sound heard at the beginning of *write* and *rhyme*. The *w* and the *h* are silent.

Best Guess
for *kn*, *gn*, or *pn* at the beginning of a word = /n/
for *wr* or *rh* at the beginning of a word = /r/

Find four words in which *k* or *g* is followed by the letter *n*. Say the words.

kite	gnat	knock	gave	kneel	grow	gnu

Look at the list of words below. What two letters begin each word? What sound do you expect the letters *kn*, *gn*, or *pn* to stand for at the beginning of each word? Now read the words.

gnarl	gnome	knee	knight	knowledge
gnarled	knapsack	kneel	knit	knuckle
gnash	knave	knelt	knob	pneumatic
gnat	knead	knife	knock	pneumonic

Read all the words aloud. Listen for the /n/ sound at the beginning of each word. Does the first letter of each word have a sound?

Now read these sentences. Notice the silent letter at the beginning of each underlined word.

1. The workers used a <u>pneumatic</u> drill to break up the concrete.

2. The tree limbs were twisted and <u>gnarled</u>.

3. The hiker had a <u>knife</u> in his <u>knapsack</u>.

4. I don't <u>know</u> if you have to <u>knead</u> this dough.

(Extra Practice, p. 213)

This lesson continues on the next page.

Find four words in which the letter *w* is followed by the letter *r*. Say the words.

wire   wrong   wait   wind   wry   written   wrap

Look at the list of words below. What two letters begin each word? What sound do you expect the letters *wr* or *rh* to stand for at the beginning of each word? Now read the words.

rhapsody	rhinoceros	rhubarb	wrath	wring
rhetorical	Rhode Island	rhythm	wreck	wrinkle
rheumatic	Rhodesia	wrack	wrench	wrist
Rhine	rhododendron	wrangle	wrestle	writhe
rhinestone	rhombus	wrap	wretched	wrung

Read all the words aloud. Listen for the /r/ sound at the beginning of each word. Does the first letter of each word have a sound?

Now read these sentences. Notice the silent letter at the beginning of each underlined word.

1. The famous <u>writer</u> is from <u>Rhode</u> Island.

2. The boys <u>wrecked</u> the living room when they <u>wrestled</u>.

3. He was <u>wrong</u> to think these <u>rhinestones</u> were diamonds.

4. I prefer poems that have definite <u>rhythm</u> and <u>rhyme</u>.

5. Sharon hung a <u>wreath</u> on the <u>wrought</u>-iron gate.

(Extra Practice, p. 213)

Silent Letters in *st*, *mb*, *mn*, and *lk*, and Silent *h*

/s/ **listen**   /m/ **climb**   /m/ **autumn**   /k/ **folk**   /silent h/ **hour**

Some words have silent letters. When the letters *s* and *t* come together in a word, usually both sounds are heard. However, sometimes *st* stands for the /s/ sound. In *listen*, the *t* is silent. Now say *climb* and *autumn*. Do you hear the /m/ sound? When *mb* and *mn* come at the ends of words, they usually stand for the /m/ sound. Usually when endings such as *-er* or *-ing* are added on, the *b* and *n* remain silent. The letter *b* is also silent in the word *debtor*.

Best Guess
for *st* within a word = /st/
Second best guess = /s/

Best Guess
for *mb* or *mn* at the end of a word = /m/

Look at each word. Where do the letters *st* appear in the word? In all these words, the second best guess is correct. Read the words.

bristle   fasten   glisten   mistletoe   rustle

Look at the words below. What sound do you expect *mb* and *mn* to stand for? Read the words.

autumn	comb	crumb	lamb	numb
climb	condemn	dumb	limb	plumber

Read all the words aloud. Listen to the sound of each word and notice the letter that is silent.

Now read these sentences. Notice the silent letter in each underlined word.

1. The child was <u>nestled</u> snugly in her bed with her toy <u>lamb</u>.

2. In <u>autumn</u> the <u>limbs</u> of the trees become bare.

3. The <u>solemn</u> guards marched in a <u>column</u>.

4. Dad will <u>bristle</u> when the <u>plumber</u> gives him the bill.

5. The doctor <u>fastened</u> a splint to her broken <u>thumb</u>.

(Extra Practice, p. 214)

This lesson continues on the next page.

When the letters *lk* follow the vowel *a* or *o*, *lk* usually stands for the /k/ sound. Do you hear the /k/ sound at the end of the key word *folk*? The letter *l* is silent. The letter *h* is sometimes silent when it comes before the vowels *e* or *o* at the beginning of a word. Say the word *hour*. Do you hear the /our/ sound? The *h* is silent.

Best Guess
for *lk* following *a* or *o* = /k/

Best Guess
for *h* followed by *e* or *o* at the beginning of a word = /h/
Second best guess = /silent h/

Now look at the words below. What letter comes before the letters *lk* in each word? What sound do you expect *lk* to stand for in each word? Read the words.

caulk   chalk   stalk   talk   walk   yolk

Look at the words below. Where does the letter *h* come in each word? What letter follows *h*? In all these words, the second best guess is correct. Read the words.

heir   herb   honest   honesty   honorable   hourly

Read all the words aloud. Listen to the sound of each word and notice the letter that is silent.

Now read these sentences. Notice the silent letter in each underlined word.

1. The umpire called a <u>balk</u> on the pitcher.

2. I <u>honestly</u> don't think I can <u>walk</u> another step.

3. <u>Folks</u> from our neighborhood love to dance the <u>polka</u>.

4. He is the <u>honest</u>-to-goodness <u>heir</u> to the throne.

5. He will <u>caulk</u> the seam between the tile and tub.

(Extra Practice, p. 214)

Letters *ph*

/f/ physical, telephone, graph

When the letters *p* and *h* come together in a word, they usually stand for the /f/ sound you hear at the beginning of *physical*. Say the words *telephone* and *graph*. Do you hear the /f/ sound in each word?

Best Guess
for *ph* = /f/

Find four words in which the letters *p* and *h* appear together. Say the words.

amphibian   picture   photograph   syphon   rupture   phlegm

Now look at the words below. Find the letters *p* and *h* in each word. What sound do you expect *ph* to stand for? Read the words.

alphabet	decipher	paragraph	pheasant	philosophy
amphetamine	gopher	phantom	phenomena	phonetic
atmosphere	hyphen	pharmacy	Philadelphia	photocopy
autograph	megaphone	phase	philanthropist	sophisticated

Read all the words aloud. Listen for the sound that the letters *ph* stand for in each word.

Now read these sentences. Notice where the letters *ph* appear in the underlined words.

1. A strong <u>physique</u> is <u>physically</u> appealing to some people.

2. The <u>pharmacist</u> filled the patient's <u>morphine</u> prescription.

3. A <u>philanthropist</u> from <u>Philadelphia</u> donated money to the school.

4. <u>Ralph</u> created a colorful <u>graph</u> on his computer.

5. We saw a <u>gopher</u> and a <u>pheasant</u> on our walk in the woods.

(Extra Practice, p. 215)

Letters *ps*

/s/ psychic

When the letters *p* and *s* come together at the beginning of a word, the *p* is silent and the two letters together usually stand for the /s/ sound. Say the word *psychic*. Do you hear the /s/ sound at the beginning of the word?

Best Guess
for *ps* at the beginning of a word = /s/

Look at each word below. What sound do you expect *ps* to stand for at the beginning of each word? The Best Guess will help you with these words. Now read the words.

psalm	psyche	psychoanalysis	psychopathic
pseudo	psychedelic	psychoanalyze	psychosis
pseudonym	psychiatrist	psychological	psychosomatic
psoriasis	psychic	psychologist	psychotherapy

Read all the words aloud. Listen for the sound that the letters *ps* stand for at the beginning of each word.

Now read these sentences. Notice the letters that begin each underlined word.

1. Leo tries to <u>psychoanalyze</u> everyone else's problems.

2. Mark Twain is a <u>pseudonym</u> for Samuel Clemens.

3. <u>Psychedelic</u> colors were popular in the 1960s.

4. Jessie is studying to be a <u>psychiatrist</u>.

5. <u>Psoriasis</u> is a chronic disease of the skin.

(Extra Practice, p. 215)

Letters *qu* and *que*

/kw/ quick, square   /k/ liquor, antique

When the letters *qu* come together at the beginning of a word, they usually stand for the /kw/ sound you hear at the beginning of *quick*. When the letters *qu* appear within a word, they may stand for the /kw/ sound heard in *square* or the /k/ sound heard in *liquor*. When the letters *que* appear at the end of a word, they usually stand for the /k/ sound heard at the end of *antique*.

Best Guess
for *qu* at the beginning of or within a word = /kw/
Second best guess for *qu* within a word = /k/

Best Guess
for *que* at the end of a word = /k/

Find four words with the letters *que* at the end. Say the words.

antique   squash   unique   mosque   quell   physique

Look at the list of words below. What sound do you expect *qu* to stand for in each word? The Best Guess for *qu* is correct. Now read the words.

antiquity	exquisite	quantity	quite	squeamish
banquet	frequent	queasy	request	squirrel
consequence	inquiry	quench	require	squirt
equality	quality	question	sequence	tranquil

In the words below, the second best guess for *qu* is the right guess.

etiquette   lacquer   mannequin   mosquito   racquet   turquoise

---

Read all the words aloud. Listen for the sound that the letters *qu* or *que* stand for in each word.

Now read these sentences. Try the Best Guesses first. If you don't recognize a word, try the second best guess.

1. She dressed as <u>Queen</u> Victoria for the <u>masquerade</u> ball.

2. What an <u>exquisite</u> <u>antique</u> table that is!

3. <u>Monique</u> is <u>statuesque</u> and <u>quite</u> lovely.

4. He applied the <u>lacquer</u> to the wood in <u>quick</u> strokes.

(Extra Practice, p. 216)

Letters *wh*

/hw/ white

When the letters *w* and *h* come together in a word, they usually stand for the /hw/ sound. Say the key word *white*. Do you hear the /hw/ sound at the beginning of the word?

Best Guess
for *wh* = /hw/

Find three words in which the letters *w* and *h* appear together. Say the words.

nowhere   anywhere   knowledge   wrestle   somewhat   always

Now look at the words below. What sound do you expect *wh* to stand for in these words? The Best Guess will help you. Read the words.

elsewhere	whale	where	whim	whisk
meanwhile	what	whether	whimper	whisker
nowhere	wheel	which	whimsical	whistle
somewhat	when	whiff	whimsy	whooping
whack	whenever	while	whine	why

Read all the words aloud. Listen for the sound that the letters *wh* stand for in each word.

Now read these sentences. Notice where the letters *wh* appear in each underlined word.

1. When did you learn to whistle?

2. I know I left my white gloves somewhere in my room.

3. On a whim, they decided to go on a whale watch.

4. The child whined and whimpered while her mother shopped.

5. This meat is somewhat undercooked.

(Extra Practice, p. 216)

EXCEPTIONS

who (hü)   whole (hōl)   whom (hüm)   whose (hüz)

Letter *x*

/ks/ box, text   /ksh/ obnoxious   /z/ xylophone

When the letter *x* comes within or at the end of a word, it usually has the /ks/ sound. Do you hear the /ks/ sound in the words *text* and *box*? When *x* is followed by the letters *ious*, *ual*, *ury*, *urious*, or *uriant*, it will have the /ksh/ sound heard in *obnoxious*. When *x* is the first letter of a word, it usually stands for the /z/ sound heard at the beginning of *xylophone*.

Best Guess
for *x* = /ks/
for *x* followed by *ious*, *ual*, *ury*, *urious*, or *uriant* = /ksh/
for *x* at the beginning of a word = /z/

Look at the words below. What letters follow the letter *x*? What sound do you expect *x* to stand for in each word? Read the words.

annex	fix	maximum	oxygen	taxi
anxious	jinx	Mexico	reflex	text
axle	luxury	mixture	relax	vexation
coax	luxurious	orthodox	saxophone	wax

What sound does *x* stand for at the beginning of the words below? Read the words.

xenophobia   xerography   Xerox   xylem   xylophone

Read all the words aloud. Listen for the sounds that *x* can stand for at the beginning, within, or at the end of a word.

Now read these sentences. Notice where the letter *x* appears in each underlined word.

1. Fred relaxed on the luxuriant green lawn.

2. The child was so obnoxious, everyone left the room.

3. We studied the xylem in the plant stem.

4. She will wax the kitchen floor to make it shine.

(Extra Practice, p. 217)

EXCEPTIONS

x-axis (eks'ak'sis)   X ray (eks'rā')

Letters *et*

/ā/ ballet

There are many words in English that have come from the French language. Some of these words end in the letters *et*. These words have kept the French /ā/ sound for *et*. The *t* is silent in these words. Say the word *ballet*. Do you hear the /ā/ sound at the end? The words *depot* and *debut* are also from the French language. The letter *t* is silent in *depot* and *debut*. *Depot* is said /dē′pō/, and *debut* is said /dā′byü/.

Best Guess

for *et* at the end of a word from the French language = /ā/

Look at the words below. They are all from the French language. What sound do you expect *et* to stand for at the end of each word? The Best Guess will help you. Now read the words.

| beret | cabaret | crochet | fillet | ricochet |
| bouquet | chalet | croquet | parquet | sachet |

Read all the words aloud. Listen for the sound that the letters *et* stand for at the end of each word.

Now read these sentences. Notice where the letters *et* appear in each underlined word.

1. The basketball court has <u>parquet</u> flooring.

2. Dinner was served <u>buffet</u> style.

3. Joey has a job waiting on tables in a small <u>cabaret</u>.

4. <u>Berets</u> are hats that are similar to tams.

5. Have you ever seen a professionally performed <u>ballet</u>?

(Extra Practice, p. 217)

Mixed Review

Practice what you have learned by reading these sentences.

1. The veterans paid honor to those who had died in the war.
2. A mosquito bit Joan on the arm.
3. The lawyers helped them come to an equitable solution.
4. Anna has not written to me in months.
5. Gnats are pesky little bugs.
6. You are not expected to answer a rhetorical question.
7. Mrs. Woo put a sachet in her bureau drawer.
8. Did the cashier who waited on you give you a receipt?
9. Concetta admired the silver brush and comb set.
10. Jerry pricked his finger on the stem of the thistle.
11. The doctor may not prescribe medicine for viral pneumonia.
12. Tina didn't realize she was talking to a mannequin.
13. The violinist made his debut at Carnegie Hall.
14. The teacher could not decipher Mark's handwriting.
15. Vivian has a unique speaking voice.
16. They went to Paris for the weekend on a whim.
17. Jon scraped his knuckles on the rough wood.
18. The weather bureau used sophisticated radar to track the storm.
19. The boss requested six Xeroxed copies of this material.
20. The ants marched in a column carrying a bread crumb.
21. The Frenchman wore his beret tilted to one side.
22. Walking is great exercise.
23. The train will arrive in the depot at six o'clock.
24. This recipe calls for four egg yolks.
25. Do you believe in psychic phenomena?

PART 6 · PROBLEM WORDS

Some words are problems because they look like other words. Other words are problems because they do not follow the rules you have studied. Part 6 has some hints that help people read problem words. See if the ideas help you.

Context

The **context** of a word is the meaning of all the words around it. Often, the context is the sentence in which you read the word. It can also be the whole paragraph. Context helps you read. It makes you expect a certain kind of word. Here is an example. Read this sentence:

I ____ my coat on a chair.

The blank tells you that something is missing. Your own sense tells you the kind of word that is missing. The word will probably say something about what you do or did with the coat. The word *put* would make sense in this sentence. A word like *left* or *dropped* would also make sense. The word *but* or *pot* would not make sense.

When you find a word you cannot read, stop and think. Look at the context. Read the next few sentences. Ask yourself what kind of word would make sense.

Reading Syllables

Something else to look for when you find a long new word is its syllables. Remember, a **syllable** is a word or word part that has one vowel sound.

With a long new word, find the first syllable by looking at the first vowel. Look at the letter just after it. Is it a consonant or a vowel? Do you see a pattern you know, like VCC or VCV? Is the first vowel in a common prefix, such as *un-* or *re-*? These questions will help you guess at the sound of the first vowel. Then look at any other letters in the syllable. Does any letter come before the first vowel? Are there two letters before the vowel? Now try to say the first syllable. Then go on to the next syllable and do the same thing.

On the next page is an example of how this works.

Let's say you cannot read the word *department* in this sentence:

Sam found a tie at the department store.

You see that the first syllable is a common beginning, *de-*. The next syllable has an *a* in it, followed by two consonants. You guess that it is a short *a* that follows the VCC rule. You guess that the next syllable follows the same rule. Now you try reading the word syllable by syllable: *de + part + ment*. You also think about what kind of store has ties. Now you can read the word.

Letter Order

Some words look like other words. The word *was*, for example, has the same letters as the word *saw*. However, the letters are in a different order. People often read the letters in the wrong order and misread the words.

How can you be sure to read letters in the right order? First, look at the vowel in a word. Then look at the letter or letters that follow it. Point to them with your pencil. Do the letters make a pattern you know, like VCC? Now try to say the vowel and the letters that follow it.

Then look to the left of the vowel. Do you see a consonant or letter team? If so, point with your pencil. Move the point to the left of the vowel. Say the sound you expect those letters to have. Then point to the vowel and say that sound. You will find that pointing at letters helps you read the words the right way.

In this lesson, you will see many pairs of words. The words in each pair are easy to mix up. Some have the same letters in a different order. Some have one or two different letters.

The letters that most people mix up are vowels in letter teams. Often the vowels are teamed with *r* or *l*. Look carefully at such teams to see if the *r* or *l* comes before or after the vowel. Try reading the words below. Try to read both words in a pair without mixing them up. If you have trouble with a word, point to its letters as you read them.

arid	raid		farm	frame
bark	brake		feel	flee
balk	black		flu	full
barn	bran		from	form
calm	clam		melt	metal

Now read these sentences. Let the context of each underlined word help you read the word.

1. Tap the <u>brakes</u> to see how they <u>feel</u>.

2. Put the <u>black</u> cow in the <u>barn</u>.

3. Would you like a <u>clam</u> roll or a tuna <u>melt</u> sandwich?

4. Use a door that has a <u>metal</u> <u>frame</u>.

5. When the dog is <u>calm</u>, it does not <u>bark</u>.

(Extra Practice, p. 218)

Go on to the next page.

Here are more pairs of words. Reading a word by itself is often harder than reading a word in a sentence. In a sentence, the context can help you. When you read a word that stands alone, you must read it carefully.

bold	blood	pealed	plead
bolt	blot	percent	present
broad	board	poured	proud
cold	clod	pulse	plus
corps	crops	quiet	quite
could	cloud	silt	slit
dairy	diary	silver	sliver
filter	flitter	sulk	skull
garb	grab	terse	trees
gild	glide	warp	wrap
gourd	ground		

If you have trouble reading any word pairs, try this: copy the word pair onto a sheet of paper. Look at the first word. Circle the vowels in it. Then draw a small arrow above the letter that follows each vowel. Now look at the other word in the pair. Find the vowel. What letter follows the vowel? What letter comes before it? Try to see how the words in each pair are different. Then try to read them again.

Now try reading some of these words in sentences. Let the context of each underlined word help you read the word.

1. I poured the dirty water onto the ground.

2. Your pulse is fast when your blood moves quickly.

3. Grab the bolt when you shut the gate.

4. I got a sliver in my finger from that board.

5. Use this form to order a new filter.

(Extra Practice, p. 218)

Here are more pairs of words for you to read.

conscious	conscience	pond	pound
dire	drier	scared	sacred
except	expect	shirk	shrink
file	life	though	tough
fired	fried	through	thorough
fury	furry	tired	tried
girl	grill	trial	trail
knee	keen	vetoed	voted

Now try reading some of these words in sentences. Let the context of each underlined word help you read the word.

1. Sam did not <u>expect</u> to get <u>fired</u> for being late.

2. We <u>tried</u> not to get too <u>tired</u>, but the <u>trail</u> was long and steep.

3. Would you like this meat <u>fried</u> or cooked on the <u>grill</u>?

4. At first, we were <u>scared</u> by the large, <u>furry</u> animal.

5. At the <u>trial</u>, the jury <u>voted</u> four times before they could agree.

(Extra Practice, p. 219)

Letter Shapes

Sometimes words are read the wrong way because one letter is read wrong. Look at the words *brown* and *drown*. They look alike except for the first letters. Their first letters are easy to mix up because *b* and *d* look alike. Everyone misreads words at some time.

To solve this problem, learn to look closely at words. Look at the pairs of words on this page, for example. Can you see how the words in each pair are different? If you look carefully and still have trouble reading these words, tell your teacher. The two of you can then work out a plan.

bony	pony	horror	honor
born	brown	hunt	hurt
brawl	drawl	hut	nut
certain	curtain	inquiry	injury
clam	claw	jam	jaw
clobber	copper	jog	job
cod	cop	mirror	minor
corn	crown	mouth	month
funny	furry	paint	plain
garter	quarter	palm	plan
germ	grew	port	prod
gold	glob	ram	raw
guilt	quilt	torch	touch

Now read these sentences. Let the context of each underlined word help you read the word.

1. Make <u>curtains</u> that match the <u>quilt</u>.

2. <u>Paint</u> only the wood and not the <u>copper</u>.

3. In the fall, the leaves turned <u>brown</u> and <u>gold</u>.

4. My <u>pony</u> grows a heavy winter coat and looks very <u>furry</u>.

5. One person had a <u>minor</u> <u>injury</u> from the crash.

(Extra Practice, p. 219)

Sight Words

Some words are hard to read because they do not follow rules you know. For example, when you see the letters *ee*, you expect the long *e* sound. In most words, you would hear it. The word *been*, though, sounds like /bin/. You do not hear a long *e*. How do you learn such words? You do not sound them out. Instead, you learn these words by sight.

Here is a list of words to learn by sight. Use the respellings and the pronunciation guide to help you say these words.

ache	(āk)	eye	(ī)
again	(ə gen')(ə gān')	father	(fä′ᵮHər)
aisle	(īl)	floor	(flôr) (flōr)
among	(ə mung')	four	(fôr) (fōr)
answer	(an'sər)	friend	(frend)
aunt	(ant)	from	(from) (frum)
backward	(bak'wərd)	front	(frunt)
beautiful	(byü'tə fəl)	gauge	(gāj)
been	(bin)	give	(giv)
blood	(blud)	glove	(gluv)
both	(bōth)	gone	(gôn) (gon)
boulder	(bōl'dər)	half	(haf)
breakfast	(brek'fəst)	have	(hav)
build	(bild)	heart	(härt)
business	(biz'nis)	height	(hīt)
busy	(biz'ē)	island	(ī'lənd)
buy	(bī)	listen	(lis'n)
ceiling	(sē'ling)	live	(liv)
color	(kul'ər)	lose	(lüz)
come	(kum)	love	(luv)
could	(kůd)	many	(men'ē)
danger	(dān'jer)	minute	(min'it)
do	(dü)	money	(mun'ē)
does	(duz)	most	(mōst)
early	(ėr'lē)	mother	(muᵮH'ər)
ever	(ev'ər)	move	(müv)

The list continues on the next page.

nothing	(nuth'ing)		the	(ŦHə) (ŦHē)
ocean	(ō'shən)		their	(ŦHer) (ŦHar)
of	(ov) (uv)		there	(ŦHer) (ŦHar)
once	(wuns)		to	(tü)
one	(wun)		tonight	(tə nīt')
other	(uŦH'ər)		toward	(tôrd) (tōrd) (tə wôrd')
people	(pē'pəl)		two	(tü)
pint	(pīnt)		view	(vyü)
police	(pə lēs')		walk	(wôk)
pretty	(prit'ē)		want	(wont) (wônt)
purpose	(pėr'pəs)		was	(woz) (wuz)
radio	(rā'dē ō)		wear	(wer) (war)
said	(sed)		were	(wėr)
says	(sez)		what	(hwot) (hwut)
sew	(sō)		where	(hwer) (hwar)
shoe	(shü)		who	(hü)
shoes	(shüz)		whom	(hüm)
should	(shůd)		whose	(hüz)
shoulder	(shōl'dər)		woman	(wům'ən)
soldier	(sōl'jər)		women	(wim'ən)
some	(sum)		won	(wun)
son	(sun)		would	(wůd)
stomach	(stum'ək)		wrong	(rông) (rong)
sugar	(shůg'ər)		your	(yůr)
sure	(shůr)			

Now read these sentences. Let the context of each underlined word help you read the word.

1. Where did you get your shoes?

2. My mother will come for two days next week.

3. Does your friend want some sugar in his coffee?

4. We will paint the room from floor to ceiling.

5. The woman said this money is for her son's lunch.

(Extra Practice, p. 220)

Mixed Review

Practice what you have learned by reading these sentences.

1. Pump the brakes when you stop on ice.
2. I need a nut that will fit on this bolt.
3. The Army Corps of Engineers built this dam.
4. Stay on the trail through the woods, and you won't get lost.
5. Here is a towel to blot up that water.
6. This mirror is so high I can't see myself in it.
7. A small, furry animal ran across the floor.
8. The quilt was made from red scraps of cloth.
9. We want to get the crops in before the storm.
10. Wear a plain white shirt and black pants.
11. I like funny movies, not horror movies.
12. This month I get five paychecks.
13. Will there be pony rides at the fair?
14. Heat up the grill before you put on the meat.
15. The hot water made your shirt shrink.
16. The silt has blocked the mouth of the river.
17. In a fire, you must try to stay calm.
18. You can have toast or bran muffins.
19. The judge made sure that the trial was fair.
20. I have never heard my dog bark.
21. The heat from the sun will melt the ice quickly.
22. Do you want to wear my black coat?
23. Try not to break the filter.
24. Pete speaks with a real drawl.
25. We both said we would leave quite early.

EXTRA PRACTICE

In this section you will find additional sentences that you may use for extra practice for each lesson. Use these sentences to sharpen the skills you are building.

Short *a*, page 16
back, bat /a/

1. You will find the <u>jazz</u> records on the top <u>rack</u>.
2. I paid the <u>cab</u> driver with <u>cash</u>.
3. <u>That</u> <u>van</u> <u>ran</u> out of <u>gas</u>.
4. At <u>camp</u> they learned to make <u>crafts</u>.
5. A <u>branch</u> fell off the <u>plant</u>.
6. We were <u>glad</u> to find the right <u>path</u>.
7. The <u>staff</u> <u>passed</u> out a <u>stack</u> of books.
8. I <u>am</u> going to take a <u>bath</u>.
9. The <u>tram</u> travels very <u>fast</u>.
10. Put the <u>crabs</u> and <u>clams</u> in a <u>pan</u>.

Short *e*, page 17
test, bed /e/

1. <u>Ten</u> <u>men</u> applied for the job of <u>chef</u>.
2. This <u>belt</u> should go with that <u>dress</u>.
3. We bought this <u>desk</u> in <u>West</u> Virginia.
4. We got <u>wet</u> <u>when</u> the rain soaked our <u>tent</u>.
5. Please <u>tend</u> to the <u>rest</u> of your chores.
6. I <u>sent</u> a <u>check</u> to the store to pay for the <u>vest</u>.
7. <u>Ed</u> got the <u>best</u> score on the <u>test</u>.
8. <u>Yes</u>, I will <u>lend</u> you <u>ten</u> dollars.
9. The <u>next</u> <u>steps</u> in the job will be easy to do.
10. At the <u>end</u> of the month, I will pay the <u>rent</u>.

Short *i*, page 18

bill, did /i/

1. Rick used all his film at the rink.
2. Last spring, we took a trip.
3. I think his zip code is 77090.
4. He put his wig in a tin box.
5. What will we serve with the roast pig?
6. Please wrap this gift with pink paper.
7. I wish I knew how he did that trick.
8. We built a fire with twigs, sticks, and pine sprigs.
9. If you sprint, you may win the race.
10. Sue's cat will hiss and flip when it sees a dog.

Short *o*, page 19

dock, top /o/

1. When did the clock stop ticking?
2. Put the pork chops in a heavy pot.
3. I did not buy this doll at that shop.
4. When Don hit the golf ball, it shot through the air.
5. Let's sit on the top of that rock.
6. Flop on the cot and take a nap.
7. An ox can't really hop.
8. Bob has the chicken pox.
9. Mr. Fox will stop to visit the stock exchange.
10. The cop must stop the plot to rob the shop.

Short *u*, page 20

must, up /u/

1. Brush some oil on the pizza crust.
2. Let's hunt for a good place to eat lunch.
3. I hit a bump and the rug fell off the truck.
4. After you bunt the ball, run to first base.
5. Please shut the trunk of the car
6. The skunk hid in a clump of weeds.
7. We must pump up the tires with more air.
8. I trust the smudge will fade if I scrub it.
9. How much money is now in the fund?
0. I have a dull pain in my thumb.

Long *a*, page 23

tale, wait /ā/

1. Shake the grain into a pail.
2. He paid his bail and got out of jail.
3. This lane leads to my front gate.
4. Is it safe to sail on that lake?
5. We came to play a game with you.
6. I have a tame snake for a pet.
7. Wake me up when the train arrives.
8. The cows will graze in the shade.
9. Write your name at the top of the page.
0. It may rain on the day of the race.

Long *e*, page 24

bead, see /ē/

1. Teal is a green shade of blue.
2. You should eat three meals a day.
3. The reef was under the sea.
4. I would like to meet the queen.
5. Serve sweet cream with the berries.
6. He split the seam in the seat of his pants.
7. Clean the sheet with soap and water.
8. A tree grew by the stream.
9. You must kneel to weed the garden.
10. We need to buy some meat for dinner.

Long *i*, page 25

hike, cried, lie /ī/

1. Please put more spice in the pie.
2. Tie the package with twine.
3. My wife will dine with us.
4. What is the price of rice today?
5. She tried to find a ripe lime.
6. We stewed the beef in white wine.
7. This tie has a green stripe.
8. I hope the bride will like this gift.
9. Dive into the pool on this side.
10. We had to drive a mile out of our way.

Long *o*, pages 26-27
hope, boat, toe /ō/

1. I <u>hope</u> you'll enjoy this <u>joke</u>.
2. Did you hear the <u>toad</u> <u>croak</u>?
3. Please don't <u>quote</u> the <u>whole</u> article.
4. <u>Joe</u> <u>broke</u> his <u>nose</u> in the football game.
5. The <u>phone</u> was ringing when I got <u>home</u>.
6. The city is <u>close</u> to the <u>coast</u>.
7. She put the <u>note</u> in the pocket of her <u>robe</u>.
8. We <u>spoke</u> to the <u>coach</u> after the game.
9. I saw a <u>doe</u> standing in the <u>road</u>.
0. Don't <u>choke</u> on a <u>bone</u>.

Long *u*, page 28
tune, suit, due /ü/ cute, cue /yü/

1. <u>Sue</u> will be away in <u>June</u>.
2. When is the <u>duke</u> <u>due</u> back from his trip?
3. <u>Use</u> a mailing <u>tube</u> to send the poster.
4. We had a picnic on top of a <u>huge</u> <u>dune</u>.
5. She wore a <u>blue</u> <u>suit</u> to the meeting.
6. <u>Jude</u> has a <u>bruise</u> on his arm.
7. Only a <u>brute</u> would be that <u>rude</u>.
8. Feed the <u>mule</u> a piece of <u>fruit</u>.
9. The <u>cruise</u> ship sailed out into the <u>blue</u> sea.
0. Is it <u>true</u> that you wrote this <u>tune</u>?

Short *a* in Words with Two or More Syllables, page 32

racket /a/

1. <u>Danny's</u> plane will be <u>landing</u> soon.
2. This morning I <u>sanded</u> the new <u>flagpole</u>.
3. Too much <u>snacking</u> might make you <u>fatter</u>.
4. Are you <u>happy</u> with your new <u>glasses</u>?
5. The two <u>classes</u> went <u>camping</u> last weekend.
6. I am <u>planting</u> several different kinds of <u>grasses</u>.
7. Put the <u>blanket</u> in the picnic <u>basket</u>.
8. I'm <u>planning</u> to make two <u>batches</u> of cookies.
9. The <u>banker</u> is <u>cashing</u> my check.
10. The <u>traffic</u> light is <u>flashing</u>.

Short *e* in Words with Two or More Syllables, page 33

dentist /e/

1. Thank you for <u>letting</u> me come to your <u>wedding</u>.
2. He <u>rested</u> his <u>elbows</u> on the table.
3. On high <u>ledges</u> you can often hear <u>echoes</u>.
4. Why are you <u>selling</u> your <u>blender</u>?
5. I am <u>mending</u> the <u>edges</u> of the napkin.
6. The <u>dentist</u> is <u>checking</u> my teeth.
7. It's a <u>blessing</u> to have such a good <u>helper</u>.
8. The club <u>members</u> are <u>renting</u> a cabin.
9. <u>Jenny</u> is <u>spending</u> too much money.
10. The snow is <u>melting</u>, so we can't go <u>sledding</u>.

Short *i* in Words with Two or More Syllables, page 34

silver /i/

1. We were <u>winning</u> the game after the first <u>inning</u>.
2. The <u>issue</u> of new <u>bridges</u> came up at the meeting.
3. The <u>singer</u> <u>whispered</u> to the band leader.
4. The <u>pillow</u> needs a <u>bigger</u> <u>zipper</u>.
5. There were <u>sixteen</u> <u>igloos</u> in the settlement.
6. <u>Billy</u> likes to play <u>cribbage</u>.
7. In the <u>distance</u> we saw the <u>drilling</u> site.
8. Thank you for <u>bringing</u> fried <u>chicken</u> to the <u>picnic</u>.
9. My <u>sister</u> works for a <u>printer</u>.
10. I seem to be <u>missing</u> my <u>slippers</u>.

Short *o* in Words with Two or More Syllables, page 35

pocket /o/

1. <u>Donna</u> went <u>shopping</u>.
2. His rude <u>conduct</u> is <u>shocking</u>.
3. Put your <u>soccer</u> shoes in your <u>locker</u>.
4. <u>Holly</u> is <u>mopping</u> the floor.
5. I'm <u>stopping</u> at the store to buy new <u>goblets</u>.
6. She hid the gold <u>locket</u> in her <u>pocket</u>.
7. <u>Robbers</u> don't <u>follow</u> the rules.
8. The baby wore a <u>cotton</u> <u>bonnet</u>.
9. The <u>potter</u> will <u>model</u> a vase out of clay.
10. <u>Polly</u> thought that the play was <u>nonsense</u>.

Short *u* in Words with Two or More Syllables, page 36

number /u/

1. The <u>tugboat</u> is not open to the <u>public</u>.
2. I don't think your <u>puppy</u> is <u>ugly</u>.
3. The <u>bumper</u> is <u>rusty</u>.
4. The <u>trucker</u> stopped for <u>supper</u>.
5. The <u>judges</u> <u>trusted</u> that the laws were fair.
6. I am <u>stuffing</u> <u>putty</u> in the cracks.
7. The <u>usher</u> told us a <u>funny</u> story.
8. Your <u>trumpet</u> is <u>under</u> your chair.
9. I was <u>lucky</u> to get the last <u>cruller</u>.
10. <u>Bunny</u> lives on the <u>upper</u> level.

Long *a* in Words with Two or More Syllables, page 37

sailor, bacon /ā/

1. I'll be <u>taking</u> you home <u>later</u>.
2. The <u>tailor</u> is <u>making</u> some <u>changes</u> in my suit.
3. The <u>Raiders</u> were <u>trailing</u> after the first half.
4. It has been <u>raining</u> <u>daily</u> for a week.
5. He <u>stated</u> his ideas <u>plainly</u>.
6. The <u>sailor</u> had a <u>painful</u> bruise.
7. She was <u>placing</u> the <u>grapefruits</u> on <u>plates</u>.
8. The <u>salesman</u> learned some <u>basic</u> skills in a <u>training</u> session.
9. I was <u>racing</u> to the <u>mailbox</u> with my letters.
10. They are <u>raising</u> the rents in many <u>places</u>.

Long *e* in Words with Two or More Syllables, page 38

seeing, beater, meter /ē/

1. The <u>beaches</u> are <u>really</u> lovely here.
2. The <u>speaker</u> started <u>sneezing</u>.
3. We were <u>seated</u> in a box at the <u>Steelers</u> game.
4. The car <u>dealer</u> <u>treated</u> us well.
5. She wore a <u>beaded</u> jacket to the <u>meeting</u>.
6. What is the <u>leading</u> <u>treatment</u> for the common cold?
7. We are <u>eating</u> <u>meatballs</u> tonight.
8. We spent the <u>weekend</u> <u>treating</u> our cats for <u>fleas</u>.
9. It was <u>freezing</u> at the <u>seashore</u>.
0. I am <u>reading</u> a book about <u>weaving</u>.

Long *i* in Words with Two or More Syllables, page 39

fiber /ī/

1. The <u>driver</u> was <u>striving</u> to stay awake.
2. The <u>mining</u> company sells <u>limestone</u>.
3. <u>Nineteen</u> <u>bikers</u> are in the race.
4. The <u>prices</u> of <u>spices</u> are going up.
5. The <u>hikers</u> were <u>riding</u> to the mountain.
6. It is <u>vital</u> to let the fruit <u>ripen</u> before you eat it.
7. She <u>wisely</u> kept <u>silent</u> during the argument.
8. The comedy <u>writer</u> had great <u>timing</u>.
9. The <u>bridal</u> party will be <u>dining</u> alone.
0. Use bleach to <u>whiten</u> the <u>fibers</u>.

Long *o* in Words with Two or More Syllables, pages 40-41

boating, bonus /ō/

1. We have <u>chosen</u> to heat our home with <u>solar</u> energy.
2. <u>Smoking</u> is not a <u>wholesome</u> habit.
3. The <u>coastal</u> plain is <u>frozen</u>.
4. We were <u>coping</u> with a traffic jam at the <u>roadblock</u>.
5. He <u>quoted</u> a <u>slogan</u> from a television ad.
6. Jim <u>showed</u> us his <u>homemade</u> <u>robot</u>.
7. The <u>toaster</u> we bought last month is already <u>broken</u>.
8. They were <u>joking</u> in the <u>coatroom</u>.
9. He <u>boasted</u> that he knew where the <u>stolen</u> goods were.
10. The <u>lonesome</u> man was <u>phoning</u> all his friends.

Long *u* in Words with Two or More Syllables, page 42

suitor, cruel, prudent /ü/   music /yü/

1. <u>Bruno</u> inspected the <u>blueprints</u>.
2. It is <u>useless</u> to argue with <u>stupid</u> people.
3. I think the Beatles' <u>music</u> is <u>super</u>.
4. The <u>union</u> has proved <u>fruitful</u> for the workers.
5. He was <u>gluing</u> together the broken <u>cruet</u>.
6. Too much salt will <u>ruin</u> the <u>strudel</u>.
7. The ship is <u>cruising</u> to <u>Cuba</u>.
8. The <u>tuba</u> is one of the <u>hugest</u> <u>musical</u> instruments.
9. <u>Susan</u> has a great sense of <u>humor</u>.
10. The <u>students</u> <u>used</u> <u>rulers</u> to measure the box.

Second Best Guess for VCV, pages 43-44

cabin /a/   metal /e/   vivid /i/   comic /o/   punish /u/

1. Adam deserves a lot of credit.
2. He had never ridden in a taxi.
3. She hung her linen skirt in the closet.
4. A lemon has acid in it.
5. The critic gave the comic a bad review.
6. Roger studied phonics in class today.
7. The legend was about a dragon.
8. He was sent to prison to be punished for his crime.
9. Seven cabins stand on the shore.
10. The robin was too timid to take seeds from my hand.

Schwa, page 45

ago, wagon /ə/

1. Susan is hopeful that the packet will arrive soon.
2. The kitten had spotted fur.
3. The teacher has given the students guidance.
4. The hinges have broken for the second time.
5. The workmen will widen the bridges.
6. The circus is coming to Scranton.
7. Put lettuce and raisins in the salad.
8. The children fell asleep ten minutes ago.
9. They have lost their balance and fallen.
10. The tip on my pencil is broken.

Vowel y, pages 46-48

sky, apply, style /ī/   tricky /ē/   gym /i/

1. Lucy sang a lullaby to the baby.
2. I will try to reply to your question.
3. Sybil works as a hair stylist.
4. I envy Sandy because she has a large family.
5. A synonym of *flying* is *soaring*.
6. Jenny needs to dry her hair before the party.
7. Most acrylic paint contains synthetic egg whites.
8. We rode our bicycles to the gym.
9. Pretty flowers will beautify the city park.
10. Tyrone Power was a dynamic movie star.

Letter Team ay, page 53

pay /ā/

1. May will display her paintings.
2. Brush your teeth twice a day to avoid tooth decay.
3. How long will the plane stay on the runway?
4. On Thursday, I finished writing my essay.
5. Don't let the puppy stray away from the yard.
6. Raymond will portray a king in the play.
7. Hurray! Friday is payday!
8. Maybe we will win the relay race.
9. It's never okay to betray a friend.
10. He sprayed the tray with a fresh coat of paint.

Letter Team *ey*, page 54

key /ē/   they /ā/

1. The <u>pulley</u> lifted the new engine off the <u>conveyor</u> belt.
2. We paid a lot of <u>money</u> for these tickets to the <u>hockey</u> game.
3. <u>They</u> moved to New <u>Jersey</u>.
4. <u>Harvey</u> is wearing a <u>paisley</u> tie.
5. I lost my house <u>key</u> somewhere in the <u>alley</u>.
6. <u>Volleyball</u> players must <u>obey</u> the rules of the game.
7. Put some <u>parsley</u> in the stuffing for the <u>turkey</u>.
8. Little Miss Muffet ate curds and <u>whey</u>.
9. The <u>survey</u> showed that many people like <u>honey</u> in their tea.
10. This <u>valley</u> is a perfect place to grow <u>barley</u>.

Letter Team *au*, page 55

cause /ô/

1. In <u>August</u>, they opened their new <u>restaurant</u>.
2. I bought a set of cups and <u>saucers</u> at the <u>auction</u>.
3. Who has the <u>authority</u> to clear the <u>launching</u> pad area?
4. Jim's nerves were <u>taut</u> during the <u>audition</u>.
5. This <u>automobile</u> has an <u>automatic</u> transmission.
6. <u>Paula</u> stayed home last night and did her <u>laundry</u>.
7. We ate <u>sausage</u> with tomato <u>sauce</u>.
8. Mother <u>taught</u> my <u>naughty</u> brother a lesson.
9. <u>Paul's</u> income tax return was <u>audited</u>.
10. My <u>daughter</u> has <u>auburn</u> hair.

Letter Team *aw*, page 56

law /ô/

1. She has <u>drawn</u> a picture of a <u>hawk</u>.
2. The rabbit <u>pawed</u> at the <u>straw</u> in the bottom of its cage.
3. The baby <u>crawled</u> across the <u>lawn</u>.
4. She folded her <u>shawl</u> and put it in her <u>drawer</u>.
5. The frightened bird let out an <u>awful</u> <u>squawk</u>.
6. <u>Thaw</u> the <u>raw</u> meat before you cook it.
7. The <u>lawyer</u> <u>saw</u> that the jury believed the witness.
8. <u>Lawrence</u> <u>scrawled</u> a quick note to his sister.
9. The <u>fawn</u> had <u>scrawny</u> legs.
10. He <u>yawned</u> as he <u>sprawled</u> on the bed for a nap.

Letter Team *ea*, pages 57-58

bead /ē/   head /e/   great /ā/

1. Are you <u>ready</u> for a <u>great</u> <u>breakfast</u>?
2. <u>Steam</u> the <u>seafood</u> in a large pot.
3. We swam in the <u>breakers</u> at the <u>beach</u>.
4. When the <u>weather</u> turns cold, the <u>leaves</u> begin to fall.
5. The <u>eagle</u> has long white <u>feathers</u>.
6. A <u>steady</u> diet of <u>steak</u> and other red <u>meats</u> is not <u>healthy</u>.
7. The <u>threat</u> of war could be ended by a <u>peace</u> <u>treaty</u>.
8. The cows grazed in a <u>pleasant</u> <u>meadow</u>.
9. I'll wear a <u>heavy</u> <u>sweater</u> <u>instead</u> of a jacket.
10. A <u>great</u> <u>teacher</u> can <u>reach</u> <u>each</u> of her students.

Letter Team *ei*, page 59

vein /ā/   **seize** /ē/

1. Eight tons of freight were loaded into the ship.
2. I received a weird message yesterday.
3. The sheik reigns over his followers.
4. Before seizing the drugs, the police kept the dealer under surveillance.
5. That is the eighth time my neighbor has borrowed my lawn mower.
6. He deceived us by feigning illness.
7. He used to have a beige leisure suit.
8. Bravely, the cowboy seized the reins of the runaway horse.
9. At the doctor's office, Bob received a shot in a vein in his arm.
10. What is the weight of that reindeer?

Letter Team *ew*, page 60

chew /ü/   **few** /yü/

1. With an ax, he hewed a large branch from the yew tree.
2. She knew that the pewter plate was valuable.
3. The stewardess brewed some fresh tea.
4. I drew a few pictures.
5. My Uncle Lewis is Jewish.
6. The child grew tired of chewing the tough meat.
7. I threw a few carrots into the stew.
8. Andrew grew four inches last year.
9. The steward offered the passengers some peanuts and cashews.
10. Last night we flew to New Jersey.

Letter Team *eu*, page 61

neutral /ü/   feud /yü/

1. Put the car in <u>neutral</u> to start it.
2. The <u>eucalyptus</u> is a kind of tree.
3. Use an acid to <u>neutralize</u> a base.
4. The clever <u>sleuth</u> solved the mystery.
5. <u>Eugene</u> is a city in Oregon.
6. "He passed away" is a <u>euphemism</u> for "He died."
7. A hydrogen atom contains no <u>neutrons</u>.
8. <u>Euphoria</u> is a feeling of great happiness.
9. It was difficult to <u>maneuver</u> when I was on crutches.
10. The author used a <u>pseudonym</u> instead of her real name.

Letter Team *ia*, page 62

media /ē′ə/   dial /ī′ə/

1. The <u>librarian</u> helped me to find a book about sports <u>trivia</u>.
2. <u>Editorials</u> often contain <u>biased</u> statements.
3. The Alps are <u>giant</u> mountains that spread across <u>Austria</u>.
4. The <u>custodian</u> cleaned the <u>cafeteria</u>.
5. <u>Sylvia</u> collects West <u>Indian</u> baskets.
6. Antibiotics are often <u>viable</u> cures for <u>bacterial</u> diseases.
7. At the <u>trial</u>, the jury heard Bob's <u>denial</u> of guilt.
8. The <u>historian</u> drew a <u>diagram</u> to explain his point.
9. We will travel to <u>Rumania</u> and <u>Bulgaria</u>.
10. I listened to a <u>dialogue</u> on the pros and cons of disposable <u>diapers</u>.

Letter Team *ie*, pages 63-64

thief /ē/   pie /ī/   diet /ī'ə/

1. The scientist tried to explain the test results.
2. Thieves have stolen my briefcase.
3. Please retrieve your collie from my garden!
4. The spies took pictures of the top-secret supplies.
5. Rosie spoke quietly with the priest.
6. A prairie is much larger than a field.
7. The lawyer believed that his client had lied.
8. Don't eat too many cookies if you're on a diet.
9. I went to the movies with my niece.
10. Kind words may shield a person from grief.

Letter Teams *igh* and *ign*, page 65

light /ī/   sign /ī/

1. The flash of lightning frightened the child.
2. The flashlight had a bright beam.
3. The teacher might give you a homework assignment.
4. These pants are too tight in the thighs.
5. The dress was highlighted by a colorful design on the sleeves.
6. The knight resigned himself to another long battle.
7. Turn right at the stop sign.
8. Last night, I was delighted to meet your sister.
9. I bought a used highchair at the consignment shop.
10. I am frightened that he might not sign the contract.

Letter Teams *oi* and *oy*, page 66
boil, boy /oi/

1. The soldiers remained <u>loyal</u> to the <u>royal</u> government.
2. During my <u>boyhood</u>, I lived in <u>Troy</u>, New York.
3. The <u>soil</u> didn't come out of my <u>corduroy</u> pants.
4. She <u>enjoys</u> doing <u>embroidery</u>.
5. Did you hear that loud <u>noise</u> in the <u>foyer</u>?
6. I'll try to <u>avoid</u> <u>disappointing</u> you.
7. The <u>employees</u> <u>joined</u> a union.
8. I am <u>annoyed</u> that you broke the <u>toy</u>.
9. <u>Roy</u> explained his <u>point</u> of view carefully.
10. I told the waiter that my <u>choice</u> for dinner was <u>broiled</u> fish.

Letter Team *oo*, page 67
school /ü/   book /u̇/

1. In the <u>moonlight</u>, we saw a <u>moose</u> wading in the lake.
2. I'm going to my <u>bedroom</u> to take a short <u>snooze</u>.
3. <u>Soon</u> the voters will <u>choose</u> a new president.
4. We <u>stooped</u> down to pet a rabbit at the <u>zoo</u>.
5. A <u>tablespoon</u> is a useful <u>cooking</u> <u>tool</u>.
6. With my <u>zoom</u> lens, I <u>took</u> a great picture of a <u>goose</u>.
7. I got a splinter in my <u>foot</u> from that piece of <u>wood</u>.
8. My grandfather went to a one-<u>room</u> <u>schoolhouse</u>.
9. The dentist was <u>looking</u> at my sore <u>tooth</u>.
10. When the weather is <u>cool</u>, wear a <u>wool</u> sweater.

Letter Team *ou*, pages 68-69

out /ou/   young /u/

1. There was some <u>trouble</u> in the <u>county</u> prison last night.
2. There were <u>about</u> twenty people lined up at the <u>counter</u>.
3. The <u>youngster</u> has <u>outgrown</u> his <u>trousers</u>.
4. He <u>shouted</u> <u>proudly</u>, "I've caught a <u>trout</u>!"
5. I <u>found</u> a bottle of <u>mouthwash</u> in the closet.
6. At the northern <u>boundary</u> of one <u>country</u> is Canada.
7. <u>Thousands</u> of fans <u>shouted</u> when Jim scored a <u>touchdown</u>.
8. I <u>doubt</u> that the <u>couple</u> can afford a new <u>couch</u>.
9. Over the <u>loudspeaker</u>, he <u>announced</u> the name of the winner.
10. We built a <u>fountain</u> in the <u>ground</u> <u>outside</u> our <u>house</u>.

Letter Team *ow*, page 70

cow /ou/   snow /ō/

1. This restaurant is <u>known</u> for its great fish <u>chowder</u>.
2. He <u>mowed</u> <u>down</u> the <u>overgrown</u> weeds.
3. I don't <u>know</u> <u>how</u> to <u>bowl</u>.
4. Is there a <u>clown</u> in the <u>show</u>?
5. The <u>downtown</u> area has <u>grown</u> <u>crowded</u> with fancy shops.
6. She spilled <u>powder</u> on her <u>gown</u>.
7. <u>How</u> much do I <u>owe</u> you for <u>towing</u> my car?
8. The <u>undertow</u> is <u>powerful</u> today.
9. The <u>crown</u> was filled with <u>glowing</u> jewels.
10. <u>Following</u> my <u>shower</u>, I dried myself with a <u>towel</u>.

Vowel *o* with Other Consonants, page 71

off /ô/

1. He made me a cup of strong coffee.
2. Frost put a glossy covering on my windshield.
3. She offered me a sandwich and a cup of broth.
4. His boss sent him to Hong Kong on a business trip.
5. The officer stopped me for going the wrong way on a one-way street.
6. Ross lost his car keys.
7. We sat down on the soft, mossy ground and had a picnic.
8. The tablecloth was too costly for my budget.
9. He was cross when he lost the Ping-Pong game.
10. We heard the wild geese honking as they flew across the field.

l-Controlled Vowels, pages 72-73

talk /ô/   wild /ī/   old /ō/

1. I told the child not to walk in my garden.
2. All of the tickets to the basketball game have been sold.
3. Use this dish to hold the salted walnuts.
4. Today the weather is mild, but yesterday it was cold.
5. The bold soldiers led a revolt.
6. Goldenrod is a wildflower.
7. I always have to pay a toll when I cross the bridge.
8. The old man loved to waltz.
9. We put a row of folding chairs against the wall.
10. Please put a halter on the wild colt.

Letter Team *ar*, pages 74-75

car /är/   care /er/   carry /ar/   dollar /ər/   war /ôr/

1. There are four quarters in a dollar.
2. Mary was careful not to spill the sugar.
3. Are you aware that Carl won an award last night?
4. I went to the market to buy a quart of juice.
5. It is warm in the cellar near the furnace.
6. Paris is a popular place to visit, but getting there is not a bargain.
7. Warren was careless and spilled the can of varnish.
8. My parents scared me when they warned me not to swim in the quarry.
9. Larry and Mary were married in March.
10. Beware of sharks in the harbor.

Letter Team *er*, pages 76-77

term /ėr/   very /er/   after /ər/   here /ir/

1. The butter will perish very quickly if it is left in a warm place.
2. These ferns will be perfect in my flower arrangement.
3. After a hearty supper, the campers felt cheerful.
4. Are you certain that this career is right for you?
5. The merchant opened a new shop on the corner of Elm Street.
6. Father said that we're going to the barber shop after dinner.
7. The weather in southern Texas is usually warmer than this.
8. Numerous germs got into the cut on my finger.
9. Hamburger and steak come from steers.
10. My brother cheered when he heard you were the winner of the race.

Letter Team *ir*, page 78

bird /ėr/   fire /īr/

1. My little girl is sick with a virus today.
2. I was irate when I learned that you had been fired.
3. Blackbeard was one of the first pirates to be captured in America.
4. The forest fire destroyed many birch and fir trees.
5. Keep stirring the sauce even if you get tired.
6. I bought a set of iron fireplace tools.
7. The circus needs to hire more clowns.
8. Thirty children came to her birthday party.
9. The fire engine has a loud siren.
10. Firm copyright laws protect against the piracy of taped movies.

Letter Team *or*, pages 79-80

for /ôr/   sorry /or/   favor /ər/   word /ėr/

1. Store the unused porridge in the refrigerator.
2. What is the normal color of her hair?
3. Before we leave for New York tomorrow, let's borrow a camera.
4. I'd like to correspond with my favorite author.
5. A game in which there is no score can be boring.
6. After he does his homework, he does chores around the house.
7. A horrible odor was coming from the garbage can.
8. Organize your thoughts before you begin work on your report.
9. At the store, I bought a humorous card to send to Mrs. Lord.
10. This morning I had the worst headache I've ever had.

Letter Team *ur*, pages 81-82

fur /ėr/   jury /ùr/
pure /yùr/   picture /ər/

1. They moved from their <u>urban</u> apartment to a <u>rural</u> farm.
2. Put your <u>purple</u> socks away in the <u>bureau</u>.
3. This <u>turban</u> is made from <u>natural</u> fibers.
4. His new job will provide him with a <u>secure</u> <u>future</u>.
5. Last <u>Thursday</u>, I was <u>injured</u> in an accident.
6. The <u>jury</u> looked at <u>pictures</u> of the victim.
7. These <u>curtains</u> do not go with my new <u>furniture</u>.
8. The <u>nurse</u> put in an <u>urgent</u> call to the doctor.
9. Did the <u>hurricane</u> do any <u>further</u> damage?
10. <u>Featured</u> on the menu was <u>turkey</u> soup with <u>turnips</u>.

Letter Team *ear*, page 83

ear /ir/   learn /ėr/   bear /er/

1. The class was <u>learning</u> about <u>Earth's</u> atmosphere.
2. In the spring, we will plant a <u>pear</u> tree <u>near</u> the garden.
3. I <u>heard</u> that you are moving away next <u>year</u>.
4. He <u>searched</u> for the missing car keys.
5. The campers were <u>fearful</u> when the <u>bear</u> <u>appeared</u>.
6. Jeff worked on the <u>yearbook</u> committee.
7. She was <u>wearing</u> a beautiful string of <u>pearls</u>.
8. We sat in the <u>rear</u> of the theater during the <u>rehearsal</u>.
9. By <u>early</u> afternoon, the plows had <u>cleared</u> most of the snow.
10. I work every other weekend to <u>earn</u> extra money.

Letter Teams *air* and *eir*, page 84

hair /er/   their /er/

1. I bought some chocolate <u>eclairs</u> at the new bakery.
2. The carpenter will <u>repair</u> the back <u>stairs</u>.
3. Prince Charles is <u>heir</u> to the British throne.
4. The ice on the windshield <u>impaired</u> my vision.
5. She has a <u>flair</u> for entertaining.
6. My sister has blond <u>hair</u> and <u>fair</u> skin.
7. We bought an antique <u>chair</u> at the <u>fair</u>.
8. She let me borrow a <u>pair</u> of skis.
9. They went to Florida for <u>their</u> vacation.
10. Can you pick me up at the <u>airport</u>?

Letter Team *ier*, page 85

happier /ē'ər/   flier /ī'ər/   pier /ir/

1. I need some <u>pliers</u> to cut the thick wire.
2. She is much <u>happier</u> since she started her new job.
3. The green sweater is <u>prettier</u> than the red one.
4. Did you call the <u>supplier</u> to order the envelopes?
5. It would be <u>easier</u> to cook the chicken in a deep <u>frier</u>.
6. The <u>fierce</u> winds knocked down the utility pole.
7. I had my ears <u>pierced</u> when I was thirteen.
8. Karen works as a <u>cashier</u> at the ice cream stand.
9. The road is much <u>slipperier</u> after it rains.
10. It is <u>rainier</u> and <u>foggier</u> on this side of the island.

Hard *c*, page 89

cape /k/

1. Have a <u>cup</u> of <u>coffee</u>.
2. My <u>uncle</u> is named <u>Carl</u>.
3. I hope the day is <u>clear</u> and <u>cold</u>.
4. Did you <u>vacuum</u> the rug?
5. A <u>decade</u> is ten years.
6. Please <u>close</u> the <u>curtains</u>.
7. That <u>cabinet</u> maker is <u>curious</u> about this wood.
8. Make sure you have the <u>correct</u> map.
9. Are your steps made of wood or <u>concrete</u>?
10. I want to go on a <u>picnic</u>.

Soft *c*, page 90

cell /s/

1. I missed the ball <u>twice</u>.
2. I like your red shoe <u>laces</u>.
3. Have a bowl of <u>cereal</u> before you go.
4. Put the rug in the <u>center</u> of the room.
5. No one may smoke <u>cigars</u> in here.
6. Those steps are <u>icy</u>.
7. My mother and father are <u>divorced</u>.
8. This <u>bracelet</u> is made of gold.
9. The light blinks if there is an <u>emergency</u>.
10. We can <u>recycle</u> these bottles.

Consonants *cc*, page 91

occur /k/   success /ks/

1. An <u>accountant</u> does my taxes.
2. Do you want <u>saccharin</u> in your tea?
3. Will you <u>accept</u> a collect call?
4. Doctors are trying to find a <u>vaccine</u> for AIDS.
5. All our rooms are <u>occupied</u> now.
6. No one was hurt in the <u>accident</u>.
7. <u>Broccoli</u> is very good for you.
8. Please list your age and <u>occupation</u>.
9. If you eat too fast, you will get <u>hiccups</u>.
10. A <u>raccoon</u> got into my trash can.

Consonants *sc*, page 92

disc /sk/   scene /s/

1. This is such a <u>scenic</u> road!
2. My best subject is <u>science</u>.
3. Turn the <u>screw</u> to the left to loosen it.
4. That movie <u>scared</u> all of us.
5. Those <u>fluorescent</u> lights make everything look green.
6. The dentist said an <u>abscess</u> caused the pain.
7. For dinner, we ordered <u>scallops</u>.
8. These <u>scissors</u> are not sharp.
9. This flower has no <u>scent</u> at all.
10. I found a red <u>scarf</u> in the parking lot.

Consonants *ch*, pages 93-94

chip /ch/   chord /k/   chef /sh/

1. You have a <u>choice</u> of three soups.
2. Please read the first <u>chapter</u> by the end of the week.
3. Be careful how you store those <u>chemicals</u>.
4. I was a <u>chaperon</u> at the last dance.
5. The <u>chef</u> wore a big white hat.
6. The town took down the lights after <u>Christmas</u>.
7. A <u>monarchy</u> has a king or a queen as the single ruler.
8. Let's go out for <u>Chinese</u> food.
9. My lips get <u>chapped</u> in winter.
10. All the <u>chocolate</u> candy was gone.

Hard *g*, page 95

game /g/

1. Your <u>garden</u> looks very pretty.
2. We have to fix the wheel on the <u>wagon</u>.
3. Just <u>grab</u> the book out of my <u>bag</u>.
4. Is the <u>glue</u> dry yet?
5. Don't <u>wiggle</u> when I'm cutting your hair.
6. She was <u>glad</u> he had done the <u>grocery</u> shopping.
7. I think the soup needs more <u>garlic</u>.
8. You will have to <u>tug</u> at that <u>gate</u>.
9. No <u>cigarettes</u> are allowed in here.
10. Use those <u>twigs</u> to start the fire.

Soft *g*, pages 96-97

age /j/

1. This soap kills germs.
2. What a large window that is!
3. Be careful with that fragile lamp.
4. Keep milk in a refrigerator.
5. That hedge needs to be cut.
6. That truck is too big to fit under the bridge.
7. How can you tell the check was forged?
8. Each book has only a few pages.
9. Three generations of men had red hair.
10. The midget horse was the size of a dog.

Consonants *gh*, page 98

ghost /g/   night /silent gh/   laugh /f/

1. You can turn left or right.
2. I hope this flight is on time.
3. Put the bread dough into two pans.
4. Make sure we have enough wood for a fire.
5. Draw a straight line under the title.
6. People said that the ghost walked around only at night.
7. A team could be six or eight players.
8. This cough is going to keep me awake.
9. The car will not fit through such a narrow gate.
10. Please turn off the light when you go.

gu + Vowels, pages 99-100

guess /g/   language /gw/

1. An <u>iguana</u> is a large lizard.
2. A strong breeze will <u>extinguish</u> the candle.
3. <u>Guava</u> jelly is nice with cream cheese.
4. <u>Fatigue</u> is your greatest worry on a long hike.
5. Alan is studying to be a <u>guidance</u> counselor.
6. Do they play in the American or National <u>League?</u>
7. Anna remembers faces, but she is sometimes <u>vague</u> about names.
8. This watch comes with a five-year <u>guarantee</u>.
9. Make sure you buy music that is written for the <u>guitar</u>.
10. Try the <u>linguini</u> with clam sauce.

ad-, page 105

admit /ad/   adore /ə d/

1. Ricardo <u>advanced</u> quickly at his job.
2. Pam signed up for an <u>adult</u> swimming class.
3. It was an <u>adventure</u> camping in the wilderness.
4. I am not <u>adverse</u> to living somewhere else.
5. Al solved the difficult <u>addition</u> problem correctly.
6. The <u>administration</u> office will be closed for a week.
7. Tina is <u>adaptable</u> to change.
8. Take my <u>advice</u> and avoid fatty foods.
9. His guilty expression was an <u>admission</u> of guilt.
10. Art is an <u>advocate</u> for the homeless.

EXTRA PRACTICE

anti- and *ante-*, page 106

antidote /an ti/   antiaircraft /an tē/

1. She lives in a huge antebellum home in Atlanta.
2. Danny takes antihistamines for his allergies.
3. There is no antitoxin for this kind of poison.
4. Suzi added antifreeze to her car's radiator.
5. The ending to that play was anticlimactic.
6. Antiaircraft scared off the enemy planes.
7. His rude behavior is antisocial.
8. The antibodies in your blood help fight infection.
9. I don't anticipate any problems with this program.
10. Ambassador Flores is waiting in your antechamber.

be- and *bi-*, page 107

become /bi/   biannual /bī/

1. Liz stood behind me in line.
2. We use our bicuspids to bite and tear at food.
3. She was happy to hear the tumor was benign.
4. They bestowed many honors on the scientist.
5. He stayed home because he was sick.
6. The cat paced back and forth beneath the bird's cage.
7. Harry writes for a bimonthly magazine.
8. I am collecting biographical data on George Washington.
9. Luisa sat between her two older brothers.
10. The bright lights bedazzled the young girl.

co -, page 108

cooperate /kō/   committee /kə/   contribution /ko/

1. I have a confession to make.
2. The artist made an elaborate costume to wear in the festival.
3. They compromised about where to go on vacation.
4. Lee helped Kim to coordinate the party.
5. My favorite actor costars in this movie.
6. She was not prepared for the consequences.
7. Dolores felt compelled to tell the truth.
8. We watched the ants taking food back to the colony.
9. The bank required collateral before giving me a loan.
10. Tom and Katy were coauthors on a children's book.

de -, ex-, and hyper-, pages 109-110

design /di/   decode /dē/   excellent /eks/

exact /egz/   hyperactive /hī pər/

1. The building was demolished after the fire.
2. She is hypersensitive about that topic.
3. There is an exception to almost every rule in grammar.
4. The exam will begin promptly at noon.
5. The leaves will decompose and become part of the soil.
6. Some hyperactive children are helped by medication.
7. Dehydration can occur quickly when you have the flu.
8. We tried not to exclude anyone from the discussion.
9. Aren't you exaggerating just a little?
10. Bob decided to take the job in New York.

il-, *im-*, *in-*, and *ir-*, page 111

illegal /il/   imbalance /im/   incomplete /in/   irregular /ir/

1. His handwriting is totally <u>illegible</u>.
2. That argument is <u>irrelevant</u>.
3. The party was an <u>informal</u> affair.
4. He was <u>immobile</u> for two months after the accident.
5. What an <u>inane</u> remark that was!
6. The judge remained <u>impartial</u> during the trial.
7. Ruth came to an <u>illogical</u> conclusion.
8. Their differences were <u>irreconcilable</u>.
9. Ed will be out of town for an <u>indefinite</u> period.
10. A magician creates magic with <u>illusion</u>.

mega-, *micro-*, and *mini-*, pages 112-113

megaphone /meg ə/   microwave /mī krō/   microscope /mī krə/

minibike /min ē/   minimal /min ə/

1. Her parents did not approve of her <u>miniskirt</u>.
2. I will heat the water in the <u>microwave</u>.
3. There was a <u>minimum</u> of damage to his car.
4. We use more <u>megawatts</u> of electricity in winter than in summer.
5. Bacteria are <u>microscopic</u> germs.
6. They performed <u>microsurgery</u> on Nancy's eye.
7. We rode the <u>minibus</u> to the downtown shopping area.
8. The doctor warned against taking a <u>megadose</u> of vitamins.
9. You can <u>minimize</u> the danger if you take simple precautions.
10. Speak clearly into the <u>microphone</u>.

non- and *per-*, page 114

nonfiction /non/   permission /pər/   permanent /pėr/

1. He will <u>perform</u> before a sell-out crowd.
2. The smell <u>permeated</u> the whole house.
3. This is a <u>nonprofit</u> organization.
4. Try to keep your <u>perspective</u> on this issue.
5. The witness committed <u>perjury</u>.
6. These glasses are <u>nonbreakable</u>.
7. Tear the paper along the <u>perforated</u> edges.
8. What <u>percentage</u> of your salary goes to taxes?
9. He advocates a <u>nonviolent</u> approach.
10. This meat is cooked to <u>perfection</u>.

poly- and *post-*, page 115

polygon /pol ē/   postpone /pōst/

1. I am enrolled in a <u>postgraduate</u> class at the university.
2. A <u>polygon</u> has three or more sides.
3. He added a <u>postscript</u> to the letter.
4. They made a <u>poster</u> advertising the dance.
5. Amy studied <u>polyesters</u> in chemistry.
6. They performed a <u>postmortem</u> on the deceased.
7. There is <u>polystyrene</u> in the insulation of many older homes.
8. Will you send me a <u>postcard</u> from Italy?
9. She had to <u>postdate</u> the check until payday.
10. A word with many syllables is <u>polysyllabic</u>.

pre- and pro-, pages 116-117

prepare /pri/   prearrange /prē/   prejudice /pre/

promote /prə/   program /prō/   promise /pro/

1. There is no precedent for this legal decision.
2. I presume you will make the necessary preparations.
3. He had a profound effect on Carol's career.
4. She aged prematurely.
5. We use propane gas to light that stove.
6. Tim has a proposition to make concerning your business.
7. Jess explained the premise of her paper.
8. Sam was put on probation by the principal.
9. The professor introduced himself to the class.
10. Can you recite the preamble to the Constitution?

re-, page 118

reappear /rē/   recover /ri/   recommend /re/

1. Please reseal the package.
2. I accept your resignation with sadness.
3. They rehearsed until after midnight.
4. The class will reenact the first moon walk.
5. Court will reconvene after lunch.
6. Do you remember her name?
7. Jan couldn't reconcile her checkbook balance.
8. The Smiths will refinance their mortgage.
9. The price on the dress was reduced by 50%.
10. She reapplied for school in the fall.

EXTRA PRACTICE

sub-, super-, and syn-, pages 119-120

subway /sub/   submerge /səb/   superman /sü pər/

synonym /sin/

1. What is the subtitle of that book?
2. She received a subpoena to appear in court.
3. Millie belongs to the synagogue on the corner.
4. They used substandard materials in the building.
5. The flood waters subsided when the rain stopped.
6. It took superhuman effort to overcome his disability.
7. He suffers from a strange, unexplainable syndrome.
8. He was arrested for subversive activities.
9. The supervisor fired the lazy worker.
10. We moved into a house in a new subdivision.

un-, uni-, and tele-, page 121

uncooked /un/   unicycle /yü nə/   telephone /tel ə/

1. The child was unharmed in the fall.
2. Americans probably watch too much television.
3. He carried the heavy box into the house unassisted.
4. This unisex shirt is unattractive.
5. The cost of the project is still undetermined.
6. We received a telegram informing us that we had won.
7. Most people are unproductive when they are tired.
8. This program will be uninterrupted by commercials.
9. The facts of the accident remain unclear.
10. His music has universal appeal.

-*able* and -*ible*, page 122
adorable, possible /ə bəl/

1. His actions were <u>questionable</u>.
2. What an <u>incredible</u> series of events!
3. This has been a <u>profitable</u> year for our company.
4. I leave you in <u>capable</u> hands.
5. I bought a dress made of <u>washable</u> silk.
6. Frank is <u>eligible</u> for a promotion in the spring.
7. Isn't Gary a <u>likable</u> fellow?
8. There was a <u>terrible</u> explosion at the chemical factory.
9. Paula is a <u>responsible</u> and <u>sensible</u> adult.
10. We live in a <u>comfortable</u> apartment in the city.

Vowel + *cy* and Vowel + *sy*, page 123
privacy, fantasy /ə sē/

1. He was in <u>ecstasy</u> over the new car.
2. We questioned the <u>legitimacy</u> of the transaction.
3. The company has a no-smoking <u>policy</u>.
4. He recognized the <u>immediacy</u> of the problem.
5. It is <u>hypocrisy</u> to call her a liar when you yourself lie.
6. You may meet someone from the <u>aristocracy</u> in London.
7. The pain in her chest is caused by <u>pleurisy</u>.
8. John used <u>diplomacy</u> when talking to his boss.
9. Estelle wanted <u>privacy</u>, so she went to her room.
10. There are laws against <u>piracy</u> on the high seas.

-age, page 124

garbage /ij/   garage /äzh/

1. He booked <u>passage</u> on the first train out of town.
2. We rented a <u>cottage</u> on the beach.
3. He answered a <u>barrage</u> of phone calls about the election.
4. Please help me carry my <u>luggage</u> upstairs.
5. Our <u>mortgage</u> payment is due on the first of the month.
6. She made a <u>collage</u> out of old family photographs.
7. Can you estimate the <u>damage</u> to my car?
8. There is a <u>shortage</u> of food in many countries.
9. I think we can <u>manage</u> without you for a week.
10. Donna will <u>massage</u> her sore muscles.

-ance and *-ence*, page 125

ambulance, difference /əns/

1. There isn't much <u>difference</u> between the two cars.
2. She receives a small <u>allowance</u>.
3. George has a lot of <u>confidence</u> in himself.
4. There is a quality of <u>elegance</u> about her.
5. I couldn't see the <u>relevance</u> of her story.
6. He had a <u>recurrence</u> of the flu.
7. Michael spoke with <u>eloquence</u> to the <u>audience</u>.
8. We bought all new <u>appliances</u> for the kitchen.
9. I don't have much <u>tolerance</u> for boring people.
10. The juggler can <u>balance</u> three boxes on his head.

-*ant* and -*ent*, page 126

important, excellent /ənt/

1. I have an <u>urgent</u> message for you.
2. The meeting covered <u>important</u> issues.
3. She looked <u>radiant</u> on her wedding day.
4. Olivia is a <u>resident</u> of New Mexico.
5. There were over two hundred <u>applicants</u> for the job.
6. The company conducted an <u>independent</u> survey.
7. What an <u>excellent</u> worker you are!
8. Children sometimes find it difficult to be <u>obedient</u>
9. Becky was promoted to <u>assistant</u> store manager.
10. He claims to be a <u>descendant</u> of Thomas Jefferson.

-*ate*, page 127

locate /āt/   pirate /it/

1. We will <u>communicate</u> through the mail.
2. A table is an <u>inanimate</u> object.
3. Is that coat <u>adequate</u> protection against the cold?
4. The inspector will <u>investigate</u> the scene of the crime.
5. The captain had to <u>navigate</u> the boat through rough waters.
6. Danielle is a <u>considerate</u> and loving daughter.
7. John will <u>narrate</u> the class play.
8. We want to use real flowers to <u>decorate</u> the float.
9. This is not an <u>appropriate</u> time to discuss the problem.
10. Children will often <u>imitate</u> their parents.

-ed, page 128

hunted /ed/   begged /d/   walked /t/

1. I <u>bumped</u> into Nicole at the mall.
2. The ice <u>melted</u> quickly in the sun.
3. Jenny <u>begged</u> her mother to let her stay up later.
4. We <u>followed</u> the parade through town.
5. He <u>reheated</u> his dinner in the microwave.
6. I've <u>saved</u> every letter that you ever wrote me.
7. His face <u>reflected</u> his happiness.
8. The rabbit <u>hopped</u> out of sight.
9. She <u>risked</u> all her money in the stock market.
10. Have you <u>tested</u> these batteries to find out if they work?

-ine, page 129

machine /ēn/   imagine /ən/

1. <u>Christine</u> sent me a get-well card.
2. Don't forget to take your <u>medicine</u>.
3. The cottage was in <u>pristine</u> condition when we arrived.
4. Anne wants to be a <u>marine</u> biologist.
5. Did you <u>determine</u> how many miles it is to the lake?
6. Here is the latest issue of your favorite <u>magazine</u>.
7. She was <u>quarantined</u> while she had scarlet fever.
8. It's hard to <u>imagine</u> what life was like without computers.
9. The doctor prescribed <u>morphine</u> for his cancer patients.
10. <u>Chlorine</u> bleach helps whiten clothes.

-*ism* and -*asm*, page 130
communism /iz əm/   sarcasm /az əm/

1. The actors felt the criticism of the play was unfair.
2. The student was suspended for plagiarism.
3. There is a lot of symbolism in religious ceremonies.
4. We discussed the commercialism of the holidays.
5. The hikers jumped over the narrow chasm.
6. Spasms in his throat made him cough.
7. The godparents held the baby during the baptism.
8. Catholicism and Judaism are religions.
9. His constant sarcasm is so annoying.
10. My enthusiasm for jazz is growing.

-*ity* and -*ety*, page 131
unity, society /ə tē/

1. I didn't see the necessity of revealing his identity.
2. The writer has a facility with language.
3. His unpleasant personality is a liability in business.
4. Propriety demands that such vulgarity be punished.
5. What a calamity it was to be without electricity!
6. She felt great anxiety until the elevator moved again.
7. Jack peeked inside the package to satisfy his curiosity.
8. Mr. Lewis has the ability to speak with clarity.
9. The vaccine provides immunity against the polio virus.
10. Charity is an admirable virtue to practice.

E X T R A   P R A C T I C E

-*ive*, page 132
active /iv/   arrive /īv/

1. Denise is a <u>defensive</u> driver.
2. Six of the beached whales did not <u>survive</u>.
3. This writing is <u>indicative</u> of his style
4. They offered a trip to Bermuda as a sales <u>incentive</u>.
5. What can you <u>derive</u> about the character from this story?
6. The candidate made a <u>provocative</u> speech.
7. The walk in the brisk air <u>revived</u> our energy.
8. The article on sailing was very <u>instructive</u>.
9. Inez <u>contrived</u> a way to get into the private meeting.
10. Mr. Kim looks <u>distinctive</u> with gray hair.

-*le*, page 133
circle /əl/   little /l/

1. They make such an attractive <u>couple</u>.
2. The baby held the <u>rattle</u> in her tiny hands.
3. He plays the <u>fiddle</u> for our annual square dance.
4. She has a <u>dimple</u> in her cheek when she smiles.
5. We walked out in the <u>middle</u> of the <u>terrible</u> play.
6. The enemy surrendered after the bloodiest <u>battle</u> of the war.
7. There is <u>ample</u> time to complete the job.
8. All that was left of the building was a pile of <u>rubble</u>.
9. The stewardess told us to <u>buckle</u> our seat belts.
10. I won't be <u>able</u> to attend your party.

-*ous*, page 134
famous /əs/

1. He is not <u>serious</u> about quitting his job.
2. The trip over the mountains was <u>perilous</u>.
3. What a <u>gorgeous</u> dress!
4. Her younger sister was often <u>jealous</u> of her success.
5. Measles is a highly <u>contagious</u> disease.
6. There is a <u>marvelous</u> new movie at the theater.
7. We are gathered together to celebrate a <u>joyous</u> event.
8. That comedian is <u>hilarious</u>.
9. The results of the experiment were <u>instantaneous</u>.
10. There are <u>numerous</u> spelling mistakes in this letter.

-*sure* and -*sual*, page 135
pleasure /zhər/   **pressure** /shər/   **usual** /zhü əl/
sensual /shü əl/

1. Can you <u>reassure</u> me that there is no danger?
2. He suffered <u>visual</u> impairment in the accident.
3. Seth is a <u>casual</u> acquaintance of mine.
4. I try not to fill up all my <u>leisure</u> time with planned activities.
5. This self-help book is a <u>treasure</u> of ideas.
6. Shirley felt <u>pressured</u> into signing the contract.
7. That is an <u>unusual</u> combination of colors and patterns.
8. <u>Measure</u> the ingredients into the mixing bowl.
9. Pat kept her <u>composure</u> even though she was embarrassed.
10. This <u>disclosure</u> will <u>ensure</u> that the criminal is convicted.

-*tion* and -*ssion*, page 136
nation, passion /shən/

1. The <u>convention</u> will be held in Toronto next spring.
2. Take a left at the <u>junction</u> of Routes 20 and 109.
3. The hockey player got a <u>concussion</u> when he fell.
4. The rack attaches to the wall with <u>suction</u> cups.
5. She suffers from <u>depression</u> during the winter.
6. Mr. Larson works for the State <u>Sanitation</u> Department.
7. We will continue this <u>discussion</u> after dinner.
8. Many people have left the teaching <u>profession</u>.
9. First <u>editions</u> of old books may be valuable.
10. She made a <u>concession</u> to her husband's wishes.

-*sion*, page 137
vision /zhən/　tension /shən/

1. Hector read the abridged <u>version</u> of the book.
2. Charlie received a <u>pension</u> from the bus company.
3. We went on a river raft <u>excursion</u>.
4. Sam approached the weird machine with <u>apprehension</u>.
5. She has a <u>compulsion</u> to wash her hands every five minutes.
6. I have trouble doing long <u>division</u> problems.
7. Dan has an <u>aversion</u> to snakes.
8. There was understandable <u>confusion</u> after the accident.
9. He improved his <u>comprehension</u> by reading more.
10. The <u>explosion</u> was a <u>diversion</u> so the prisoners could escape.

Endings after *ti-*, *ci-*, *sci-*, pages 138-140

partial /shəl/ patient /shənt/ electrician /shən/
appreciate /shē āt/ conscience /shəns/ conscious /shəs/

1. My associate recommended you as a good lawyer.
2. The dietician outlined healthier eating habits for Joe.
3. He made a partial payment on his bill.
4. The ring is a precious reminder of my grandmother.
5. She bought white Venetian blinds for the bathroom windows.
6. I'm not superstitious about black cats.
7. The X-ray technician wore a blue lab coat.
8. The ambassador initiated the talks between the two countries.
9. Is this the most efficient way to gather the information?
10. His conscience told him not to lie.

-ture and *-tual*, page 141

nature /chər/ actual /chü əl/

1. He presented a factual report to the finance committee.
2. Our family has many holiday rituals.
3. This drink is a mixture of lemonade and orange juice.
4. The doctor suspected the patient's appendix had ruptured.
5. The museum has the sculptures of many modern artists.
6. There would be an eventual end to the stormy weather.
7. Stand straight to improve your posture.
8. This movie features two great stars.
9. The aperture of the camera lets in light.
10. I admire his intellectual approach to life.

Silent Letters in *kn*, *gn*, *pn*, *wr*, and *rh*, pages 145-146

know, gnaw, pneumonia /n/

1. The mouse gnawed at the cheese.
2. I knew her when she was a child.
3. Knock before turning the knob.
4. He just recovered from a bout with pneumonia.
5. A pneumatic drill is a powerful tool.
6. Sue gnashes her teeth while she sleeps.
7. One kind of bacteria is called pneumococcus.
8. The knight knelt at the feet of the king.
9. A gnome is a small, elf-like creature.
10. We ordered gnocchi at the Italian restaurant.

write, rhyme /r/

1. Please hand me the monkey wrench.
2. Kathy made a delicious strawberry-rhubarb pie.
3. I fractured my wrist in a wretched fall.
4. Does a poem always have to rhyme?
5. A rhinoceros has wrinkled, leathery skin.
6. The rhododendron bushes are in full bloom.
7. The writer described her trip to Rhodes.
8. She wore a rhinestone bracelet on her wrist.
9. We took a boat cruise on the Rhine River in Germany.
10. Good dancers have good rhythm.

Silent Letters in *st*, *mb*, *mn*, and *lk*, and Silent *h*, pages 147-148

listen /s/   climb /m/   autumn /m/

1. The plumber fastened the joints together.
2. My fingers are numb from the cold.
3. We'll have to hustle to make the bus.
4. Never condemn someone without knowing the facts.
5. He kissed his wife under the mistletoe.
6. The wind rustled through the trees.
7. There were four white lambs and one black one.
8. Add up the figures in this column.
9. Cora hastened to tell us what happened.
10. There are crumbs all over the table.

folk /k/   hour /silent h/

1. She planted an herb garden.
2. Ms. Lewis wrote on the board with chalk.
3. Art received an honorary degree from my college.
4. I like the yolk firm in my fried eggs.
5. Did he balk when you told him what to do?
6. The fox stalked the rabbit in the woods.
7. The new-born baby wanted to be fed hourly.
8. Is that your honest opinion?
9. Denise can talk on the phone for hours.
10. Rob walked downtown to get a paper.

Letters *ph*, page 149
physical, telephone, graph /ph/

1. They share the same carefree philosophy of life.
2. Karen is going through a rebellious phase.
3. The little girl recited the alphabet for her parents.
4. There is a hyphen in Jon-David's name.
5. An eclipse is an astronomical phenomenon.
6. The apartment had a dingy atmosphere.
7. We saw *The Phantom of the Opera* on Broadway.
8. I try to phone home once a week.
9. Physiology is the study of how living things function.
10. Liz used a megaphone to shout directions to the crowd.

Letters *ps*, page 150
psychic /s/

1. A psalm is a sacred poem or hymn.
2. Dr. Albert is a psychiatrist.
3. Alicia claims to have supernatural psychic powers.
4. Kathy learned a lot about herself through psychotherapy.
5. The two leaders were engaged in psychological warfare.

Letters *qu* and *que*, page 151

quick, square /kw/   liquor, antique /k/

1. Hal <u>requested</u> that we meet him at seven.
2. This <u>plaque</u> commemorates 30 years service in the company.
3. The ring was made of silver and <u>turquoise</u>.
4. The monster in that film was horribly <u>grotesque</u>.
5. Helen owns an <u>exquisite</u> gold necklace.
6. Stop <u>quarreling</u> and make up.
7. That glass of cold water <u>quenched</u> my thirst.
8. They opened a dress <u>boutique</u> in the mall.
9. The <u>equator</u> passes through Ecuador in South America.
10. There is alcohol in beer, wine, and other <u>liquors</u>.

Letters *wh*, page 152

white /hw/

1. <u>Whooping</u> cough is a serious childhood disease.
2. <u>Why</u> is the train late?
3. Did you get a <u>whiff</u> of her perfume?
4. <u>Whisk</u> the egg <u>whites</u> in a large bowl.
5. The baby is fascinated by the <u>wheels</u> on the toy truck.
6. I like to vacation <u>anywhere</u> that it is hot and sunny.
7. Sam was <u>somewhat</u> annoyed with his younger brother.
8. This cup of soup <u>whetted</u> my appetite.
9. I don't know <u>whether</u> to leave or stay.
10. He is fourteen and beginning to get <u>whiskers</u>.

Letter *x*, page 153

box, text /ks/   obnoxious /ksh/   xylophone /z/

1. Jack's son attends <u>Xavier</u> College in Ohio.
2. Could you phone for a <u>taxi</u>?
3. A <u>luxury</u> hotel is being built on the beach.
4. Here is a <u>Xerox</u> copy of the bill-of-sale.
5. Sneezing and yawning are natural <u>reflexes</u>.
6. Can't I <u>coax</u> you to join us for lunch?
7. We saw a red <u>fox</u> dash across the road.
8. Peter took <u>saxophone</u> lessons for six years.
9. The material on the couch has a rough <u>texture</u>.
10. The dialogue in the movie has strong <u>sexual</u> overtones.

Letters *et*, page 154

ballet /ā/

1. <u>Crochet</u> needles are much smaller than knitting needles.
2. They stayed in a ski <u>chalet</u> in a small village in the mountains.
3. <u>Filet</u> mignon is a tender and expensive cut of beef.
4. Gary brought his wife a beautiful <u>bouquet</u> of flowers.
5. The guests played <u>croquet</u> on the lawn.

Letter Order, pages 159-161

First list, page 159

1. Draw a line from left to right.
2. The bulk of the work was done by the donkey.
3. You can't flee from yourself.
4. Nancy is home in bed with the flu.
5. The athlete ate bran and other healthful foods.
6. Make sure you pack each box so it is full.
7. The police planned a raid on the store.
8. Please fill out this form.
9. Water is hard to find in an arid land.
10. My grandparents still work their farm.

Second list, page 160

1. This room is quite hot.
2. Six plus three equals nine.
3. These coins are made of silver.
4. I am one hundred percent happy with this car.
5. Two people could fit in the back seat.
6. Add a sliver of cheese to this hot dog.
7. The nurse checked my pulse.
8. At the present time, the company has full employment.
9. Look for a quiet place to read.
10. That is not a storm cloud, so don't worry.

Third list, pages 160-161

1. Do you want your eggs <u>fried</u>?
2. The children were <u>scared</u> of the dark.
3. A bad <u>conscience</u> can keep you awake nights.
4. Have you <u>tried</u> to fix it yourself?
5. No one will be <u>fired</u> for making an honest mistake.
6. Do not <u>expect</u> me to arrive before noon.
7. The church altar was filled with <u>sacred</u> objects.
8. I was so <u>tired</u> that I slept very well.
9. We soon became <u>conscious</u> of the animals around the fire.
10. Everything was dry <u>except</u> for his shoes.

Letter Shapes, page 162

1. Make <u>certain</u> that the door is locked.
2. We have plum <u>jam</u> and strawberry preserves.
3. Look at the big <u>claws</u> on that bear!
4. The way she talked, with a <u>drawl</u>, made her sound relaxed.
5. In this play the <u>curtain</u> closes only at the end.
6. My <u>jaw</u> <u>hurts</u> from chewing so much.
7. Let's have fried <u>clams</u> for dinner.
8. Help me <u>hunt</u> for the button I lost.
9. I <u>jog</u> home from my <u>job</u> every day.
10. The doctor promised that the X ray would not <u>hurt</u>.

Sight Words, pages 163-164

1. Your <u>mother</u> is a <u>pretty</u> <u>woman</u>.
2. We can <u>both</u> have a sandwich and a <u>half</u>.
3. The <u>soldier</u> would not <u>answer</u> any questions.
4. My <u>friend</u> has <u>gone</u> to <u>live</u> in another town.
5. Papa made a <u>business</u> out of going to the post office.
6. You <u>sure</u> have a <u>beautiful</u> <u>view</u> from your window!
7. My <u>son</u> and <u>four</u> other boys are helping me.
8. <u>Come</u> <u>early</u> when we are not so <u>busy</u>.
9. <u>Once</u> a day, he <u>says</u> how lucky he is.
10. It will break my <u>heart</u> if you go.

APPENDIX

CONSONANT TEAMS

Consonant teams are pairs or groups of consonants. Many consonant teams blend the sounds of the consonants together. For example, the letters *sp* at the beginning of *spell* sound like /s/ and /p/ blended together. Other consonant teams make new sounds. For instance, the letters *ch* in the word *much* have a sound that is different from the sounds of the *c* and *h*.

Consonant teams can be found at the beginnings of words, as in *drip*. They can be found in the middle of words, as in *wishful*. They can be found at the ends of words, as in *patch*. Knowing the sounds that consonant teams have will help you read words. Look at the consonant teams below. Key words will help you know what sounds the consonants stand for in words.

These letter teams are often found at the beginnings of words.

bl	**bl**ue	pr	**pr**ess	shr	**shr**imp
br	**br**own	qu	**qu**ick	spl	**spl**ash
ch	**ch**op	sh	**sh**op	spr	**spr**ing
cl	**cl**ip	sk	**sk**ip	squ	**squ**awk
cr	**cr**op	sl	**sl**ip	str	**str**ing
dr	**dr**ip	sm	**sm**ell	th	**th**is, **th**in
fl	**fl**ag	sn	**sn**ap	tr	**tr**ee
fr	**fr**om	sp	**sp**ell	thr	**thr**ee
gl	**gl**ad	st	**st**op	tw	**tw**in
gr	**gr**een	sw	**sw**ing	wh	**wh**at
pl	**pl**ay	scr	**scr**eam		

These letter teams are often found at the ends of words.

ch	su**ch**	mp	sto**mp**	rk	wo**rk**
ck	ba**ck**	nch	lu**nch**	rn	tu**rn**
ct	fa**ct**	nd	ba**nd**	rt	pa**rt**
ft	le**ft**	ng	ri**ng**	sk	de**sk**
ld	to**ld**	nk	tha**nk**	st	be**st**
lk	mi**lk**	nt	we**nt**	tch	wa**tch**

More consonant teams are subjects of lessons in this handbook.

PREFIXES

A **prefix** is a word part that is added to the beginning of a word or word root. When a prefix is added, it usually changes the word's meaning. For example, when the prefix *un-* is added to the word *happy*, it changes the meaning of the word to "not happy."

Knowing many prefixes helps you read and understand a large number of words. Look at the prefixes below. See how many you already know, then try to learn some of the ones you do not know.

Prefix	Meaning	Examples
a-, ab-	on, away from	aboard, absent
ad-, at-	to, toward, attached	adhesive, attach
ambi-, amphi-	both	ambidextrous, amphibian
ante-	before	anteroom, antedate
anti-	against	antiwar, antisocial
auto-	self	automobile, autograph
be-	cause to be, to be	belittle, befriend
bene-, bon-	good, well	benefit, bonus
circum-	around	circumference, circumstance
co-, col-, com-, con-, cor-	together, with	cooperate, collect, combine, convention, correspond
contra-, counter-	against, opposite	contradict, counterproposal
de-	down, from	descend, detract
demi-, hemi-, semi-	half	demitasse, hemisphere, semicircle
dis-	opposite	dishonest, disagree
e-, ex-	out, out of	eject, exhaust
equi-	same, equal	equator, equidistant
extra-	outside of	extraterrestrial, extraordinary
fore-	front, before	forearm, foretell
hyper-	above, beyond	hyperactive, hyperspace
hypo-	beneath, below	hypodermic, hypothalamus
il-, im-, in-, ir-	not	illegal, immature, inexpensive, irregular
im-, in-	in, into, within	imprint, inject

Prefix	Meaning	Examples
inter-	among, between	international, interrupt
intra-	within	intramural, intrastate
magna-, magni-	great, large	magnanimous, magnify
mal-	wrong, bad	malfunction, malevolent
maxi-	large	maximize, maximum
mega-	large	megaphone, megaton
micro-	small	microphone, microscope
mid-	middle	midsummer, midway
mini-	small	miniskirt, minimum
mis-	wrong	mistake, mistrial
multi-	many	multiply, multinational
non-	not, reverse of	nonpaying, nonessential
ob-, op-	not, against	object, opposite
omni-	all, every	omnibus, omnipotent
over-	over, beyond	overhear, overdose
para-	beside, different	paragraph, paradox
per-	through, throughout	perfect, perfume
peri-	around, outer	perimeter, periscope
poly-	many	polygon, polygamy
post-	after	postpone, postdate
pre-	before	prefix, precaution
pro-	forward, in favor of	project, proponent
re-	back, again	return, review
sub-, sup-	under	submarine, support
super-	over, above	supervise, superficial
syn-, sym-, syl-	same, with, together	synonym, symmetrical, syllable
tele-	far, distant	television, telescope
trans-	across	transpose, transatlantic
ultra-	over, extreme	ultrasonic, ultraconservative
un-	not	unable, unbeaten

Number prefixes are on the next page.

Number Prefix	Meaning	Examples
uni-, mono-	one	unicycle, monologue
bi-, du-	two	bicycle, duet
tri-	three	tricycle, triplets
quadr-, quart-	four	quadruplets, quarter
pent-, quint-	five	pentagon, quintuplets
hex-, sex-	six	hexagon, sextuplets
hept-, sept-	seven	heptagon, September
oct-	eight	octave, octopus
non-, nove-	nine	nonagenarian, November
dec-, deci-	ten	decade, decimal
cent-, centi-	hundred	century, centimeter
milli-	thousand	millimeter, million
kilo-	thousand	kilometer, kilowatt

SUFFIXES

A **suffix** is a word part that is added to the end of a word or word part. Suffixes can change a word's part of speech as well as its meaning. The word *act*, for instance, is a verb. When the suffix *-or* is added, the word becomes *actor*, a noun that means "someone who acts."

Knowing suffixes helps you read and understand many words. Look at the suffixes below and on the next page. See what part of speech each suffix forms and how many suffixes you already know. Then try to learn some of the ones you do not know.

Suffixes	Part of Speech/Meaning	Examples
-able, -ible	(adj.) able to, capable	available, edible
-acy	(noun) state of being	accuracy, diplomacy
-age	(noun) state of being	marriage, pilgrimage
-al	(adj.) related to, like	natural, magical
-ance, -ence	(noun) state, quality of	annoyance, confidence
-ant, -ent	(adj.) being like	ignorant, evident
	(noun) person who	assistant, student
-an, -ian	(noun) relating to, practicer of	Mexican, electrician
-ar, -er, -or	(noun) person who	beggar, worker, actor
-ary, -ery, -ory	(noun) person who, place, trade	missionary, winery, reformatory
-ate	(verb) make happen	liberate, activate
	(adj.) related to, like	literate, considerate
-cle, -cule	(noun) small	particle, molecule
-dom	(noun) state of	kingdom, freedom
-ectomy	(noun) removal of	appendectomy, tonsillectomy
-ed, -d	(verb) forms past tense	stamped, walked
-en	(verb) make happen	quicken, tighten
	(adj.) made of	wooden, golden
-er	(adj.) more than	redder, happier
-ern	(adj.) belonging to	eastern, northern
-est	(adj.) the most	finest, bluest
-ful	(adj.) full of	graceful, beautiful
-fy	(verb) to make	magnify, terrify
-hood	(noun) state of	motherhood, childhood

Suffixes	Part of Speech/Meaning	Examples
-ic, -ical	(adj.) related to	poetic, comical
-ine	(adj.) like, related to	feminine, marine
-ion, -sion, -tion	(noun) state of being	champion, revision, education
-ique, -esque	(adj.) like, kind	unique, statuesque
-ish	(adj.) like	foolish, bluish
-ism, -asm	(noun) system, process of	baptism, spasm
-ist	(noun) person who	chemist, pianist
-itis	(noun) inflammation of	appendicitis, tonsillitis
-ity	(noun) state of being	necessity, legality
-ive	(adj.) inclined to	active, conclusive
-ize	(verb) to make	realize, standardize
-less	(adj.) without	hopeless, careless
-like	(adj.) like	childlike, lifelike
-ly	(adj.) like	friendly, scholarly
	(adv.) in the manner, to the extent	poorly, constantly
-ment	(noun) state of being	government, fragment
-ness	(noun) state of being	kindness, worthiness
-ous	(adj.) full of, being	nervous, monstrous
-some	(adj.) tending to	tiresome, fearsome
-ure	(noun) action, process	erasure, failure
-ward	(adj.) in the direction of	backward, upward

WORD ROOTS

A **word root** is the part of a word that gives the word its main meaning. Every word has a root. In the word *porter*, *port* is the root. The root *port* comes from Latin, and it means "carry." A *porter* is "one who carries."

Many words in our language come from Greek or Latin roots. Sometimes, the root has another word part added, as in *import* or *portable*. By knowing word roots, you can begin to read and understand many other words. Look at the roots below and on the next two pages. This is a list of only *some* of the roots used by the English language. Try to learn a few new ones each day.

Root	Meaning	Examples
acr, aci	bitter, acidic	acrid, acid
alter	other	alternate, alternative
amor	love	amorous, enamored
annu, enni	year	annual, biennial
anthr	humanity	anthropology, philanthropy
arch	chief, ruler, first	monarch, archaeology
aqua	water	aquarium, aquamarine
aster, astr	star	asterisk, astronaut
aud	hear	audience, audible
auto	self	automatic, autograph
bibl	book	bibliography, bible
bio	life	biology, biography
brev	short	abbreviate, brevity
cap	head	capital, captain
card, cord	heart	cardiac, cordial
carn	flesh, meat	reincarnation, carnivorous
cede, ceed, cess	go, yield	recede, exceed, recession
cep, ceiv	take, hold	receptive, receive
chron	time	chronic, synchronize
cid, cis, scis	kill, cut	homicide, incision, scissor
civ, cit	citizen	civic, citizen
cogn	know, think	recognize, cognition
corp	body	corporation, corpse
crat	rule, member	democrat, aristocrat
cred	believe	credit, incredible

Root	Meaning	Examples
cruc, crux	cross	crucify, crux
cycl	circle	bicycle, cyclone
dei	god	deity, deify
dem	people	democracy, epidemic
dict	say, tell	dictate, dictionary
duc, duct	lead	educate, induction
dyn	force, power	dynamite, dynamic
eco	outer, surrounding	ecology, ecosystem
ego	I	egocentric, egotist
fac	make, do	factory, facsimile
fid	trust, loyal	fidelity, fiduciary
fort	strong	fortitude, fortify
gen	kind, birth, species	genes, generation
geo	earth	geography, geology
gram	drawing, writing	diagram, grammar
graph	write, writing	graphology, autograph
hydr	water	hydrant, dehydration
loc	place	location, relocate
log, logy	speech, study	dialogue, biology
man, manu	hand	manipulate, manual
meter	measure	thermometer, kilometer
migr	move	migrate, immigrant
mis, mit	send	missile, transmit
mob, mot, mov	move	mobile, motive, move
mut	change	mutation, commute
ortho	straight	orthodontist, orthodox
pac	peace	pacifist, pacify
pater, patr	father	paternal, patriarch
path, pass	disease, feeling	pathology, passion
ped, pede	foot	pedal, centipede
ped	child	pediatric, pediatrician
phil, phile	love	philanthropy, bibliophile
phys	body, nature	physician, physical

Root	Meaning	Examples
phob	fear	phobia, claustrophobic
phon	sound	phonograph, telephone
photo	light	photograph, telephoto
port	carry	portable, import
psych	mind, soul	psychic, psychology
quer, ques, quir	ask, seek	query, question, inquiry
rid, ris	mock, make fun of	ridicule, derision
rupt	break	interrupt, rupture
secu, sequ	follow	consecutive, sequence
sed, sess	sit	sedentary, session
sens, sent	feel	sensitive, resent
sci	know	science, conscience
scop	see	microscope, telescope
scribe, script	write	transcribe, scripture
sign	mark	signal, signature
son	sound	sonar, unison
solv, solu	loosen, free	absolve, solution
spec	look at	spectacle, respect
tact, tang	touch	contact, tangible
temp	time	contemporary, tempo
terr	earth	terrace, territory
therm	heat	thermostat, thermal
tract	drag, pull	tractor, contract
urb	city	urban, suburban
vac	empty	vacation, vacuum
ven, vent	come	convene, prevent
ver	truth	aver, verify
	turn	divert, inversion
vid, vis	see, sight	video, vision
volv	roll	revolve, involve
voc, vok	call	vocal, invoke
zoo	animal	zoology, zoospore

INDEX

INDEX